Grammy's Gourmeting Again

By: Pat Ziegler

ISBN: 978-0-9839674-1-5

FORWARD

It's funny how life takes different twists and turns. After my first cookbook, **Grammy's Gourmet**, was printed, I called a friend of mine, Eileen Tucker (who I have known since 1974), to tell her I had the books she had ordered. Eileen was working for a sorority house, Kappa Kappa Gamma, at the University of Cincinnati. She was running the kitchen there every day as they were short a cook. So as you look through this new collection of recipes, you will see quite a few that have the source as the "Kappa House".
Yes, that became my most recent profession.
Being at the Kappa House was fun. Although, I have been accused by some as corrupting the next generation of young ladies; I met some really great people. While mentioning some of the girls and not others would be unfair, I have to tell you that one of the girls told me she gained 20 pounds by eating my desserts. The one person I do want to mention is Katie Kampman. She is the house mom and together we discovered a bunch of yummy recipes.
My most wonderful daughter-in-law, Julie Schilling, is editing this work. She laughs at me because I don't know how to spell. Isn't 40 spelt *fourty*?? After all if 4 is *four*, then doesn't it make sense that 40 should be **fourty**? Don't confuse with the facts.
Hopefully there won't be too many spelling errors. Julie is also endeavoring to make sure the directions are understandable. She knows I'm not good a following instructions while I cook. Recipes are just a suggestion to how things are to be made. I usually find something to change to improve them (of course, that's just one girl's opinion).
As with my first cookbook; many thanks to all the wonderful recipes that were given to me for this volume. Two of my granddaughters age 6 & 8 at the time even contributed. It's great to know so many wonderful cooks and share all the fantastic food.
You will notice that some of the recipes were from a different era. One calls for ten cents worth of beef and five cents worth of cheese. My maternal grandmother was the best cook I have ever known. As my older brother likes to remind me, I will never be as good in the kitchen as she was. I do believe I solved the mystery of the amount of beef and cheese.

All proceeds are being donated to: Red Wolf Sanctuary, P.O. Box 202, Rising Sun, IN. 47040. 812-438-2306. www.redwolf.org Red Wolf is a non-profit, taxdeductible organization that is dedicated to the preservation and continued existence of North American wildlife. Email at info@redwolf.org or look for them on Facebook. Any questions, comments, suggestions can be sent to me at patziegler1@comcast.net.

Bon Apatite

As you open this cookbook, be prepared to be completely and utterly stuffed after making one of Pat's recipes! This cookbook is filled with recipes to please any appetite. I first met Pat in late 2009 when she began cooking at my sorority house, Kappa Kappa Gamma, at the University of Cincinnati. I quickly learned that she was a woman with a story. Kappa sisters living in the house could spend hours sitting in the kitchen talking, laughing and hearing Pat's crazy, but ever so thrilling stories, all while she cooked delicious meals for us. Her outspoken and tell-it-how-it-is attitude was contagious! With her great stories and delicious meals, Pat quickly became a favorite in Kappa's Kitchen. Over the last two years, Pat has become more than just a cook in Kappa's kitchen; she is a great friend, role model, story-teller and best of all, a GREAT cook! Enjoy all of Pat's wonderful cookbooks and be sure to always go back for seconds!   --

Katy A. Freeman

"I am confident that every recipe in this book will "stir" you to "mix" it up in your own kitchen. Cougs is the most skillful chef I know and is as sweet as her pies. This is a cookbook you will always want to include in your entertaining menus."

Ashley Robertson/Kappa Kappa Gamma

GRAMMY'S GOURMETING AGAIN

Appetizer
Antipasto Wreath
Benno's Open House Dip
Bread Dip
Chilled Berry Soup
Corn Salad
Guacamole Hummus
Layered Nacho Dip
Taco Dip
Tomato Brushetta

Beverage
Frozen Virgin Margaritas
Fruit Cooler
Strawberry Lemon Ade

Breads
Buttermilk Nut Bread
Chocolate Banana Softies
Strawberry Bread

Breakfast
Baked Peanut Butter Oatmeal
Cinnamon Toast
Crockpot Oatmeal
French Toast Strata
Ham and Cheese Omelet Roll

Dessert
Banana Cake
Blueberry Cheese Danish
Butter Crumb Coffee Cake
Carmel Corn with Nuts
Cashew Brittle
Cherry Cobbler
Chocolate Candied Apples
Chocolate Frosted Peanut Butter Cupcakes
Chocolate Royale Cheesecake Squares
Cookies and Cream Pudding
Dulce de Leche Cheesecake
Dutch Babies
Frito Candy
Lemon Bars
Peanut Butter Cup Cheesecake

Peanutty Squares
Pecan Caramels
Peppermint Cookie Cups
Pie Crust
Pumpkin Butterscotch Cookies
Pumpkin Cheesecake
Pumpkin Cookies
Pumpkin Dessert
Snickers Salad
Sticky Toffee
Turtle Bars

Entree
Bacon Cheeseburger Pizza
Baked Spaghetti
Baked Ziti Supreme
Beef Burgundy over Noodles
Beef Stew
Beef Stroganoff
Beef and Bean Torilla Bake
Black Bean Pasta
Bow Ties with Chicken and Asparagus
Bruschetta Chicken Bake
Buffalo Chicken Tenders
Chicken Cordon Bleu Pizza
Chuckwagon Chili Mac
Colorful Chicken and Rice
Confetti Spaghetti
Creamy Pasta with Bacon
Farm House Chicken Dinner
Fiesta Taco Casserole
Four Cheese Baked Ziti
Four Cheese Bow Ties
Frisch's Pizza
Fusille with Spicy Pasta
Garlic Butter Shrimp
Hamburger Pie
Italian Pasta Bake
Italian Spaghetti
Lasagna Mexican
Macaroni Chicken Dinner
Meatball Dunkers
Mexicali Cornbread Casserole
Mexican Casserole Made Easy
Pasta with Fresh Tomatoes; Basil and Chicken
Pepperoni Pizza

Pepperoni Pizzazz
Pork Chops and Rice
Pot Roast
Saucy Pasta
Sausage Bread Pudding
Shrimp with Pesto and Spaghetti
Southwest Frito Pie
String Cheese Manicotti
Sun-Dried Tomato and Olive Pesto
Taco Cornbread Pizza
Taco Mac
Taco Salad
Talapia with Pesto
Tomato Cobbler

Miscellaneous
Balsamic Vinegarette Salad Dressing
Cracked Peppercorn Dressing
Creamy French Dressing
Ranch Dressing
Sun-Dried Tomato Hummus
Veggie Dip
Vinaigrette Dressing

Salad
Bean and Barley Salad
Bow Tie Salad
Colorful Corn Salad
Colorful Mediterranean Chickpeas
Creamy Macaroni Salad
Four Berry Spinach Salad
Fruit Salad with Poppy Seed Dressing
German Potato Salad
Grape Salad
Greek Salad
Pasta Salad
Three Bean Salad
Tomato Mozzeralla Salad
Tropical Salad

Sandwich
Grilled Beef and Provolone Sandwiches
Pizza Sandwich Loaf
Pulled Chicken Sandwiches
Sloppy Joe

Sauces
Guacamole - Quickly
Guacamole - Scratch
Mango Tango Salsa

Side Dish
Applesauce - Homemade
Baked Rice
Barbecue Green Beans
Broccoli with Walnuts & Cherries
Creamed Spinach
Creamy Smashed Potatoes
Easy Cheesy Potatoes
Escalloped Corn
Green Beans
Green Beans With Colored Peppers
Gypsy Goulash
Mac & Cheese
Pecan Crumble Sweet Potato Casserole
Roasted Tomatoes
Vegetable Casserole

Snack
Chocolate Mint Wafer
Garlic Snacks
Glazed Pecans
Iced Nuts
Peanut Butter Popcorn
Popcorn Nut Crunch
Spiced Nuts
Spiced Pecans
Spicy Oyster Crackers
Spicy Vanilla Pecans

Soup
Beef Barley Soup
Chicken Noodle Soup
French Onion Soup
Mock Turtle Soup
Old Fashioned Turkey Soup
Santa Fe Cheese Soup
Sweet Potato Soup
Sweet Potato and Black Bean Chili
Tomato Cream Soup
Vegetable Soup

Antipasto Wreath

Source: Pat
Origin:

Type: Miscellaneous
Category: Appetizer

Quantity	Measure	Item
1	8 ounce	Cream Cheese
¾	Cup	Cup Chopped Pepperoni
1/2	Cup	Grated 3 blend cheese
1/4	Cup	Black olives, chopped
2	Tablespoon	Chopped fresh basil
6	Tablespoon	Chopped roasted red pepper, divided
1	Tablespoon	Parsley
		Crackers of choice

Instructions:

Mix cream cheese, pepperoni, grated cheese, olives, chopped basil and 1 tablespoon peppers until well blended.

Shape into a 16" log, wrap in plastic wrap.

Refrigerate 1 hour or until firm enough to handle.

Form into a wreath shape on large plate.

Top with remaining peppers and parsley.

Serve with crackers.

Applesauce - Homemade

Source: Becki Droege
Origin:

Type: Fruit
Category: Side Dish

Quantity	Measure	Item
20		Apples - peeled and chopped
1	Cup	Splenda or sugar
1	Teaspoon	Cinnamon
1/2	Teaspoon	Nutmeg
2	cups	Water
2	Tablespoon	Lemon juice

Instructions: Stir all together in a crock pot and slow cook on low for 7 hours.

Bacon Cheeseburger Pizza

<table>
<tr><td>**Source:** Kappa House
Origin:</td><td>**Type:** Meat
Category: Entree</td></tr>
</table>

Quantity	Measure	Item
½	Pound	Ground beef
1	Small	Onion
1		12" pizza crust; baked
1	8 ounce	Can Pizza Sauce
6	Strips	Bacon
20		Dill pickles
2	Cup	Shredded mozzarella cheese
2	Cup	Shredded cheddar cheese
1	Teaspoon	Pizza or Italian seasoning

Instructions:

Cook beef and onion over medium heat until meat is no longer pink; drain and set aside

Place pizza crust on an ungreased 12" pizza pan.

Spread with pizza sauce.

Top with beef mixture, bacon, pickles and cheese.

Sprinkle with pizza seasoning.

Bake at 450 for 8-10 minutes or until cheese is melted.

Yield: 8 slices

Baked Peanut Butter Oatmeal

Source: Becki
Origin:

Type:
Category: Breakfast

Quantity	Measure	Item
3	Cup	Quick cooking oats
1/2	Cup	Brown sugar
1	Cup	Milk
2	Tablespoon	Butter, melted
2		Egg
2	Teaspoon	Baking powder
2	Teaspoon	Vanilla
1/2	Cup	Peanut butter
		Warm milk

Instructions:
Mix all ingredients together (except milk) and stir well

Spread in a greased 9x13 pan

Bake at 350 for 20-25 minutes

For crunchy cook a few minutes longer

Serve with warm milk poured over top.

Baked Rice

Source: Beth Lake
Origin: Unknown

Type: Meatless
Category: Side Dish

Quantity	Measure	Item
1 1/4	Cup	Rice
1	Cup	Sugar (possibly more if needed)
1/2	Teaspoon	Vanilla
		Milk

Instructions:

Put rice, sugar and vanilla in a large baking dish and cover with milk. Bake at 350 until done. Stir often so top will not burn and get to dry. Add more milk as needed to keep moist. Rice will double in size as it cooks. Raisins can be added if desired.

Baked Spaghetti

Source: Lauri Ziegler Bishop		**Type:** Meat
Origin:		**Category:** Entree

Quantity	Measure	Item
1	Cup	Onion
1	Cup	Green pepper
1	Tablespoon	Butter
1	28 ounce	can Tomatoes with liquid; cut up
1	4 ounce	can Mushroom; drained
2	Teaspoon	Oregano
1 1/2	Pound	Ground beef; browned and drained
12	Ounce	Spaghetti; cooked and drained
2	Cup	Shredded cheddar cheese
1	Can	Cream of mushroom soup; undiluted
1/4	Cup	Water
1/4	Cup	Grated Parmesan cheese

Instructions:

In a large skillet, sauté onion and green pepper in butter until tender.

Add tomatoes, mushrooms, and oregano.

Add ground beef.

Simmer uncovered for 10 minutes.

Place half of spaghetti in a greased 13 x 9 baking dish.

Top with half of the meat mixture.

Sprinkle with 1 cup of cheddar cheese.

Repeat layers.

Mix soup and water until smooth; pour over casserole.

Sprinkle with Parmesan cheese.

Bake, uncovered, at 350 for 30-35 minutes or until heated thru.

Baked Ziti Supreme

Source: Becki Droege
Origin:

Type: Meat
Category: Entree

Quantity	Measure	Item
1	Pound	Ground beef
1	Pound	Italian sausage
28	Ounce	Pasta sauce
2	cups	Mozzarella
3	cups	Tube-shaped macaroni, cooked
1	Cup	Parmesan cheese
1		Onion

Instructions:

Preheat oven to 350

Cook beef, sausage and onion until browned

Pour off fat

Stir in pasta sauce, 1/2 mozzarella and macaroni

Place in a 3-quart baking dish

Sprinkle the rest of the mozzarella and add the parmesan

Bake for 30 minutes

Balsamic Vinaigrette Salad Dressing

Source: Pat	**Type:** Dressing	
Origin: Italy	**Category:** Miscellaneous	

Quantity	Measure	Item
1 1/2	Cup	Olive Oil
1	Cup	Balsamic Vinegar
1/4	Cup	Grated Parmesan or Romano Cheese
2	Teaspoon	Salt
1	Teaspoon	Onion powder
1/4	Teaspoon	Pepper
1/2	Teaspoon	Dry mustard
1/4	Teaspoon	Garlic Powder
1	Tablespoon	Sugar

Instructions:

Mix all ingredients and pour into a glass jar.

Refrigerate several hours and shake well before using.

Variations: I use fresh garlic

Banana Cake

| Source: | Type: Cakes |
| Origin: German | Category: Dessert |

Quantity	Measure	Item
1	Cup	Butter, softened
2	Cup	Sugar
3		Eggs, beaten
1	Teaspoon	Vanilla
1	Cup	Mashed bananas
1	Teaspoon	Baking soda
1	Cup	Buttermilk
1	Teaspoon	Baking powder
3 1/2	Cup	Flour
1/4	Teaspoon	Salt

Instructions:

Cream butter and sugar.

Beat in eggs and vanilla.

Blend in mashed bananas.

Dissolve soda in buttermilk and set aside.

In a separate bowl sift together baking powder, flour and salt.

Blend dry ingredients into banana-egg mixture alternately with buttermilk.

Beat well.

Pour into a 9 x 13 inch pan and bake at 350 for 30-35 minutes or until a toothpick comes out clean.

Barbecue Green Beans

Source: Renee Caldwell
Origin:

Type: Vegetable
Category: Side Dish

Quantity	Measure	Item
4-5	Can	Green Beans
1	Package	Bacon
1	Medium	Onion; chopped
1	Cup	Ketchup
1/2	Cup	Brown sugar
1/2	Cup	Water

Instructions:

Fry bacon; set aside.

Add onions, ketchup, sugar and water to bacon grease,; bring to boil.

Simmer 10 minutes. Put over top of green beans in 9x13 dish.

Crumble bacon on top.

Bake at 350 for 45 minutes.

Bean and Barley Salad

Source: Kappa		**Type:** Vegetable
Origin:		**Category:** Salad

Quantity	Measure	Item
3/4	Cup	Barley - quick cooking
1	16 ounce	can Kidney beans, rinsed and drained
1	15 ounce	can Black bean; rinsed and drained
1	11 ounce	can Whole kernel corn; drained
1		Sweet red pepper; finely chopped
6		Green onions; chopped
1/2	Cup	Cilantro
		Dressing
3/4	Cup	Olive oil
1/3	Cup	Red wine vinegar
2	Clove	Garlic`
1 1/2	Teaspoon	Chili powder
3/4	Teaspoon	Ground cumin
1/2	Teaspoon	Crushed red peppers
1/4	Teaspoon	Pepper

Instructions:

Prepare barley per package directions.

Transfer to bowl; stir in beans, corn, red pepper, onion and cilantro.

In small bowl combine the dressing ingredients.

Pour over salad and toss to coat.

Chill until serving.

Beef and Bean Tortilla Bake

Source:		**Type:** Meat
Origin: Mexico		**Category:** Entree

Quantity	Measure	Item
1	Pound	Ground Beef
1	15 ounce	can Black Beans
1	15 ounce	can Pinto Beans
1	14.5 ounce	can Stewed tomatoes
1	Envelope	Taco Seasoning
2/3	Cup	Water
3/4	Cup	Cheddar Cheese
3		Spinach flavored flour tortilla cut in half, then cut crosswise into 1/2" wide strips

Instructions:

Brown ground beef; drain.
Stir in black beans, pinto beans, tomatoes, taco seasoning and water.
Cook until heated through.
Stir in 1/2 cup of cheese In 8" square baking dish spread 2 cups of beef mixture.
Top with 1/2 tortilla strips.
Add 1/2 remaining beef mixture, then remaining tortillas, then rest of meat.
Bake uncovered for 30 minutes at 350.
Sprinkle with remaining cheese and bake 5 more minutes or until cheese is melted.

Variations: If you can't find spinach flavor-flour tortillas substitute another flavor or use plain white.

Beef Barley Soup

Source: Pam Elliott   **Type:** First Course
Origin: US   **Category:** Soup

Quantity	Measure	Item
12	ounces	Beef or lamb stew meat; cut into 1 inch cubes
1	Tablespoon	Cooking oil
4	14oz. can	Beef broth
1	Cup	Chopped onion - large
1/2	Cup	Chopped celery
1	Teaspoon	Dried oregano or basil, crushed
1/4	Teaspoon	Black pepper
2	Clove	Garlic minced
1		bay Leaf
1	Cup	Frozen vegetables
1	14 1/2 ounce	Diced tomatoes; undrained
1	Cup	Sliced peeled parsnips, or cubed peeled potatoes
2/3	Cup	Quick cooking barley

Instructions:

In a Dutch oven brown meat in hot oil.

Stir in broth, onion, celery, oregano, pepper, garlic, and bay leaf.

Bring to boil; reduce heat.

Simmer, covered for 1 1/2 hours for beef (45 minutes for lamb).

Stir in frozen veggies, undrained tomatoes, parsnips and barley.

Return to boiling; reduce heat. Simmer covered, about 15 minutes more or until meat and veggies are tender.

Discard bay leaf.

Slow- cooking directions:

Substitute regular barley for quick cooking barley.

In a large skillet brown cubed beef in hot oil.

Drain off fat. In a 5 or 6 quart slow cooker combine beef and remaining ingredients.

Cover and cook on low-heat setting for 8 or 10 hours or on high-heat setting for 4 or 5 hours.

Beef Burgundy over Noodles

Source: Kappa House
Origin: US

Type: Meat
Category: Entree

Quantity	Measure	Item
1/2	Pound	Stew meat
2	Tablespoon	Diced onion
2	Teaspoon	Butter
1 1/2	Cup	Fresh mushroom
3/4	Cup	Dry red wine
1/4	Cup	Water
3	Tablespoon	Minced parsley
1		Bay leaf
1		Whole Clove
1/4	Teaspoon	Salt
1/8	Teaspoon	Pepper
1	Tablespoon	Flour
1 1/2	Cup	Hot cooked egg noodles

Instructions:

In non stick skillet, brown beef and onion in butter over medium heat.
Add the mushrooms, wine, 1/4 cup water, 2 tablespoons parsley, bay leaf, clove, salt and pepper.
Bring to a boil.
Reduce heat; cover and simmer for at least 1 hour or until beef is tender.
Combine flour with 2 tablespoons water until smooth; stir into beef mixture.
Bring to a boil; cook and stir for 2 minutes or until thick.
Discard bay leaf and clove.
Serve over cooked noodles.
Sprinkle with remaining parsley.

Variations: Can use boneless sirloin steak, cut in 1/4" strips. Also can use beef broth instead of red wine.

Beef Stew

Source:	**Type:** Meat	
Origin: US	**Category:** Entree	

Quantity	Measure	Item
1	Tablespoon	Oil - vegetable or olive
1	Pound	Stew meat
3	Cup	Water
1/2	Teaspoon	Salt
1/8	Teaspoon	Pepper
2	Medium	Carrots
1	Large	Unpeeled baking potato; cut into 1 1/2 in pieces
1	Medium	Green pepper
1	Medium	Stalk Celery
1	Small	Onion
1		Bay Leaf
1/2	Cup	Cold Water
2	Tablespoon	Flour

Instructions:

Brown stew meat in oil until all sides are brown.

Add water, salt and pepper.

Bring to boil, reduce heat just enough for that mixture bubbles gently.

Cover and cook for 2 - 2 1/2 hours or beef is tender.

Stir in Remaining ingredients except cold water and flour.

Cover and cook about 30 minutes longer.

Remove bay leaf. Whisk cold water and flour.

Gradually stir into beef mixture.

Heat to boiling,

Boil until mixture thickens.

Beef Stroganoff

Source: Grandma Burger
Origin:

Type: Meat
Category: Entre

Quantity	Measure	Item
1 1/2	Portion	Beef cut in one inch cubes, floured and seasoned
3	Tablespoon	Fat
2	Medium	Onions
1	Clove	Garlic minced or 1/4 teaspoon garlic salt
1	Teaspoon	Worcestershire sauce
2	Tablespoon	Tomato ketchup
1/2	Cup	Water
1	4 ounce	Can button mushrooms
3/4	Cup T	hick dairy sour cream or buttermilk
		Noodles or rice

Instructions:

Flour the meat cubes in mixture of flour, salt and pepper.

Melt fat in skillet, add meat cubes and brown, add the onion rings and finely minced garlic; cook and stir on medium heat until rings are yellow.

Return meat cubes to skillet; add the Worcestershire sauce, catsup, water and the liquid from the canned mushrooms.

Cover and simmer (liquid should not boil but merely "quiver" until meat pieces are completely tender- about 2 hours or more.

Five minutes before serving stir in mushrooms and sour cream or buttermilk.

Add more salt if needed.

Serve hot over cooked noodles or rice.

Benno's Open House Dip

Source: Becki
Origin: Mexico
Type: Dips & Salsas
Category: Appetizer

Quantity	Measure	Item
1	8 oz. pkg	Shredded Sharp Cheddar Cheese
1	16 oz.	Sour Cream
1	Box	Knorr' Vegetable Soup Mix
		Pickled Jalapeno Peppers - chopped fine
		Tortilla Chips

Instructions:

Thoroughly mix everything but cheese.
Add cheese but don't mix too much.
Chill for a few hours.
Remove from fridge about 20 minutes before serving

Black Bean Pasta

Source: Kappa House	**Type:** Pasta
Origin:	**Category:** Entree

Quantity	Measure	Item
9	Ounce	Fettuccine uncooked
1 3/4	Cup	Portobello mushrooms; sliced
1	Tablespoon	Olive oil
1	Clove	Garlic
1	15 ounce can	Black beans; rinsed and drained
1	14.5 ounce	can Diced tomatoes
1	Teaspoon	Rosemary
1/2	Teaspoon	Oregano
2	Cup	Fresh Spinach

Instructions:

Cook fettuccine per package directions.

In large skillet, sauté mushrooms in oil. add garlic and cook 2 minutes longer.

Stir in black beans, tomatoes, rosemary and oregano.

Cook and stir until heated through.

Stir in spinach until wilted.

Serve over fettuccine.

Blueberry Cheese Danish

Source: Becki Droege		**Type:** Fruit
Origin:		**Category:** Dessert

Quantity	Measure	Item
1	Can	Blueberry pie filling
2	Can	Crescent rolls
1	8 ounce	Cream Cheese
1/2	Cup	Confectionary sugar
1		Egg

Instructions:

Spread 1 crescent rolls in 9 x 13 pan.

Bake 5 minutes at 350.

Mix chesse, sugar and egg.

Spread over warm crescent rolls.

Pour blueberries on top of cheese mixture.

Lay 2nd can of crescent rolls on top.

Bake at 350 for 30 minutes.

Cool 4 hours or overnight.

Sprinkle sugar on top.

Cut into squares.

Bow Tie Salad

Source:	**Type:** Pasta	
Origin:	**Category:** Salad	

Quantity	Measure	Item
8	Ounce	Bow Tie Pasta uncooked
1/3	Cup	Chicken or vegetable broth
3	Clove	Garlic
1	15 ounce	can Black beans, rinsed and drained; divided
1/2	Cup	Cilantro
3	Tablespoon	Lemon Juice
2	Tablespoon	Olive Oil
1	Tablespoon	Tomato Paste
1 1/2	Teaspoon	Oregano
1/4	Teaspoon	Salt
1/2	Teaspoon	Pepper
1	Medium	Zucchini, cut in half lengthwise and sliced
1	Medium	Sweet Red Pepper, chopped
1	Medium	Green Pepper, chopped
1/3	Cup	Red Onion

Instructions:

Cook pasta according to directions.
Rinse with cold water and drain; set aside.
In a small saucepan bring broth and garlic to boil.
Reduce heat and simmer uncovered for 5 minutes.
Cool slightly.
Transfer to food processor or blender.
Add 1/4 cup black beans, oil, tomato paste, oregano, salt and pepper.
Cover and process until smooth.
In large serving bowl stir pasta, zucchini, peppers, onion, beans and paste mixture from processor.
Toss gently to coat.
Cover and refrigerate until ready to serve.

Bow Ties with Chicken and Asparagus

Source:	**Type:** Pasta
Origin:	**Category:** Entree

Quantity	Measure	Item
4	Cup	Uncooked bow-tie pasta
1	Pound	Fresh Asparagus
1	Tablespoon	Oil
1	Pound	Chicken breasts - boneless, skinless
1	8 ounce	Mushrooms
2	Clove	Garlic
1	Cup	Chicken Broth
1	Tablespoon	Cornstarch
4	Medium	Green Onions
2	Tablespoon	Chopped fresh basil
1/4	Cup	Parmesan cheese.

Instructions:

Cook pasta per box instructions.

Wash asparagus and cut in 1" pieces.

Heat oil in skillet; add chicken and cook for 2 minutes.

Stir in asparagus, mushrooms and garlic.

Cook 6-8 minutes stirring occasionally until chicken is no longer pink and veggies are tender.

In small bowl, gradually stir broth into cornstarch.

Stir in onion and basil.

Stir cornstarch mixture into chicken mixture.

Cook and stir 1 to 2 minutes or until thicken and bubbly.

Season with salt.

Toss with pasta.

Sprinkle with cheese.

Bread Dip

Source: Becki Schilling
Origin:

Type: Dips & Salsas
Category: Appetizer

Quantity	Measure	Item
8	Ounce	Cream cheese; softened
1/2	Cup	Butter; softened
1/2	Teaspoon	Dry mustard
1/2	Cup	Sour cream
2	Teaspoon	Paprika
1/2	Teaspoon	Salt
1	Tablespoon	Caraway seed
1	Tablespoon	Minced onion

Instructions:

Mix well. Serve in Bread bowl.

Broccoli with Walnuts & Cherries

Source: Kappa House	**Type:** Vegetable
Origin:	**Category:** Side Dish

Quantity	Measure	Item
2	Bunch Broccoli,	cut into florets (about 6 cups)
1/2	Cup	Walnuts; chopped
6	Clove	Garlic
2	Tablespoon	Olive oil
1/3	Cup	Dried Cherries
1/4	Teaspoon	Salt
1/4	Teaspoon	Crushed red pepper flakes

Instructions:

Steam broccoli.

In skillet sauté walnuts and garlic in oil until garlic is tender.

Stir in the cherries, salt, pepper flakes and broccoli; toss to coat.

Bruschetta Chicken Bake

Source: Kappa House
Origin: US

Type: Meat
Category: Entree

Quantity	Measure	Item
1	14 1/2 ounce	Diced Tomato
6	Ounce	Stove Top Stuffing mix for chicken
1/2	Cup	Water
2	Garlic	cloves
1 1/2	Pound	Boneless, skinless chicken breasts; cut into bite size pieces
1	Teaspoon	Dried Basil
1	Cup	Mozzarella Cheese

Instructions:

Preheat oven to 400.

Place tomatoes with their liquid in medium bowl.

Add stuff mix, water and garlic.

Stir until stuffing is moistened.

Place chicken into 13 x 9 baking dish; sprinkle with the basil and cheese.

Top with stuff mixture.

Bake 30 minutes.

Buffalo Chicken Tenders

Source: Kappa House
Origin:

Type: Meat
Category: Entree

Quantity	Measure	Item
3	Pound	Chicken tenders
		Buttermilk
		Onion powder
		Garlic powder
		Frank's hot sauce
3	Bottles	Wing sauce; to your taste

Instructions:

Put chicken tender in a dish.

Cover with buttermilk; sprinkle with onion and garlic powder; add Frank's hot sauce and refrigerate overnight.

Take chicken tenders out of buttermilk and into 9 x 13 dish.

Cover with wing sauce

Bake for a minimum of 2 hours at 325.

Butter Crumb Coffee Cake

Source:	**Type:** Cakes
Origin:	**Category:** Dessert

Quantity	Measure	Item
2	Cup	Flour
1	Teaspoon	Baking soda
1	Cup	Sugar
1/2	Cup	Butter
1		Egg
1	Teaspoon	Vanilla
1	Cup	Sour cream

Instructions:

Crumble topping:

Stir together 1 cup flour and 1/2 cup sugar.

Cut in 1/2 cup butter to resemble coarse crumbs

Sift together flour and baking soda; set aside.

In a large bowl, beat together the sugar, butter, egg and vanilla until smooth.

Alternately, add flour mixture and sour cream to beaten mixture.

Mix until smooth.

Pour batter into greased 10 x 15 pan.

Sprinkle crumbles on top.

Bake in 350 oven about 20 minutes or until toothpick comes out clean.

Buttermilk Nut Bread

Source: Grandma Burger
Origin: Unknown

Type: Loaf
Category: Breads

Quantity	Measure	Item
1 1/4	Cake	Flour
3/4	Teaspoon	Salt
3/4	Teaspoon	Soda
1 1/2	Teaspoon	Baking soda
1	Cup	Whole wheat flour
1	Cup	Walnuts - chopped
2		Eggs
1/2	Cup	Sugar
2	Tablespoon	Butter
1/3	Cup	Molasses
1	Cup	Buttermilk

Instructions:

Mix and sift flour, salt, soda and baking powder.

Add whole wheat flour and walnuts.

Mix well. Beat eggs and stir in sugar, melted butter, molasses and buttermilk.

Combine the two mixtures and beat until smooth.

Pour into buttered load pan and bake in moderate oven (350) for about 50 - 60 minutes.

Carmel Corn with Nuts

Source: Pat		**Type:** Candy
Origin: US		**Category:** Dessert

Quantity	Measure	Item
10	Cup	Popped popcorn
1	Cup	Packed brown sugar
1/2	Cup	Butter
1/4	Cup	Dark corn syrup
1/4	Teaspoon	Salt
1/4	Teaspoon	Baking soda
1/2	Cup	Mixed nuts

Instructions:

Place Popcorn in a large bowl: set aside.

In a large heavy saucepan, combine the brown sugar, butter, corn syrup, and salt.

Cook over medium heat, stirring occasionally until mixture read 238 (soft ball stage).

Remove from heat; stir in baking soda (mixture will foam).

Quickly pour over popcorn and mix well; stir in nuts.

Transfer to two greased 13 x 9 "baking pans.

Bake at 200 for 45 minutes, stirring once.

Remove from pans and place on waxed paper to cool.

Break into clusters.

Cashew Brittle

Source: Pat
Origin: US

Type: Candy
Category: Dessert

Quantity	Measure	Item
1	Tablespoon	Butter
1	Cup	Butter
2	Cup	Sugar
1	Cup	Light corn syrup
1	Cup	Water
2 1/2	Cup	Unsalted cashew halves
1/4	Teaspoon	Baking soda

Instructions:

Butter 15 x 10" pan.

In a large saucepan, combine the sugar, corn syrup and water.

Bring to a boil, stirring constantly.

Reduce heat; cut remaining butter in cubes and carefully stir into syrup.

Cook and stir until a candy thermometer reads 280 (soft crack stage).

Add nuts; cook and stir until thermometer reads 295.

Remove from heat; stir in baking soda.

Immediately pour into prepared pan.

Cool: break into pieces

Cherry Cobbler

Source: Grandma Burger
Origin:

Type: Fruit
Category: Dessert

Quantity	Measure	Item
2 1/2	Cup	Cherries - unsweetened, canned or cooked
1	Cup	Sugar
1/4	Teaspoon	Almond extract
1	Tablespoon	Corn starch
1 1/2	Cup	Flour
3	Teaspoon	Baking powder
1	Tablespoon	Sugar
1/2	Teaspoon	Salt
1/3	Cup	Crisco
1/2	Cup	Milk
1		Egg - beaten
2	Tablespoon	Sugar

Instructions:

Place cherries in greased pan.

Mix 1 cup sugar, corn starch and almond extract.

Sprinkle on top of cherries

Put the cherries in oven to warm while mixing topping.

Sift together flour, baking powder, 1 tablespoon sugar and salt.

Cut into Crisco until coarse crumbs,

Add milk and egg; stir until flour is just moistened (do not over mix).

Spread dough over warm cherries.

Sprinkle with 2 tablespoons of sugar

Bake at 400 for 35-40 minutes.

Chicken Cordon Bleu Pizza

Source: Kappa House		**Type:** Meat
Origin:		**Category:** Entree

Quantity	Measure	Item
1	13.8 ounce	Pizza crust tube
1	Cup	Alfredo Sauce
1/4	Teaspoon	Garlic Salt
1	Cup	Shredded Swiss Cheese
1 1/2	Cup	Cubed fully cooked ham
10		Breaded Chicken nuggets cut into 1/2" pieces
1	Cup	Shredded Mozzarella

Instructions:

Unroll dough onto greased 10 x 15 pan; flatten dough and build up around the edges.

Bake at 425 for 8-10 minutes or until lightly browned.

Spread Alfredo sauce; sprinkle with Swiss Cheese.

Top with ham and chicken, and Mozzarella.

Bake 8-10 minutes or until golden brown and cheese is melted.

Chicken Noodle Soup

Source: Kappa House	**Type:** First Course	
Origin: US	**Category:** Soup	

Quantity	Measure	Item
6	cups	Chicken Broth
1	Pound	Boneless, skinless Chicken thighs
1	Cup	Celery
1	Cup	Onion
1	Cup	Carrots cut into bite size pieces
1	Large	Parsnip, peeled and chopped
1	Teaspoon	Minced garlic
1		Bay Leaf
1/4	Teaspoon	Pepper
2	Cup	Uncooked medium egg noodles
1/4	Cup	Fresh Dill

Instructions:

Put broth, chicken, celery, onion, carrots, parsnip; garlic, bay leaf and pepper in large sauce pan.

Cover and bring to a boil.

Reduce heat and simmer for 25 minutes or until chicken is cooked and veggies are tender.

Discard bay leaf.

Remove chicken to a plate to cool slightly.

Add noodles to soup; cover and simmer 10 minutes or until tender.

Shred chicken.

Add to soup along with dill.

Variations: Can easily use breast of chicken or turkey.

Chilled Berry Soup

Source: Kappa House
Origin: US

Type: Fruit
Category: Appetizer

Description: Although this recipe has soup in the title, it really can be served in a small glass as a very light dessert or served on a warm afternoon. The consistency will remind you of a fruit smoothie. This needs to be thoroughly chilled so prepare at least 3 hours in advance.

Quantity	Measure	Item
1	Quart	Fresh berries (your choice)
1/3	Cup	Ginger Ale
1/4	Cup	Milk
1/3	Cup	Sugar
1	Tablespoon	Lemon juice
1	Teaspoon	Vanilla extract
1	Cup	Sour cream

Instructions:

Place berries in a food processor and puree.

Add Ginger Ale, milk, sugar, lemon juice and vanilla.

Cover and process until blended.

Pour into large bowl and whisk in sour cream.

Chill several hours.

You can reserve some berries for garnish.

Chocolate Banana Softies

Source: Becki
Origin:
Type: Fruit
Category: Breads

Quantity	Measure	Item
1 1/2	Cup	Flour
1	Teaspoon	Baking powder
1/2	Teaspoon	Salt
1/3	Cup	Butter, softened
1/3	Cup	Sugar
1/3	Cup	Light brown sugar
3		ripe Bananas
1		Large Egg
1	Teaspoon	Vanilla
1	Cup	Milk chocolate chips
1/2	Cup	Coarsely chopped walnut

Instructions:

Preheat oven to 375

Place flour, baking powder and salt in a small bowl & combine

Beat butter, sugar and brown sugar in large bowl until light and fluffy

Beat in banana, egg and vanilla

Add flour mixture

Beat on low speed until well blended

Stir in chips and walnuts

Dough will be very soft

Drop on lightly greased cookie sheet

Bake 10-13 minutes or until edges are golden brown

Stand for a couple minutes before moving to wire racks to cool completely

Chocolate Candied Apples

Source: Mycah Rose Droege
Origin:

Type: Candy
Category: Dessert

Quantity	Measure	Item
		Apples
4	Ounce	Chocolate
1/8	Teaspoon	Cinnamon
24	Ounce	White Chocolate
6		Craft sticks
		Wax paper

Instructions:

Remove stems from apples

Insert craft sticks

Put chocolate and cinnamon into a bowl and microwave for 1-2 minutes

Coat each apple with chocolate mixture

Place on wax paper

Put white chocolate into another bowl and microwave for 1 minute

Drizzle over apples with spoon

Chocolate Frosted Peanut Butter Cupcakes

Source:	**Type:** Cakes
Origin:	**Category:** Dessert

Quantity	Measure	Item
1	Package	Yellow cake mix
3/4	Cup	Peanut butter
3		Eggs
1 1/4	Cup	Water
1/4	Cup	Canola oil
1 2/3	Cup	Semisweet chocolate chips
1/2	Cup	Heavy cream
1/2	Cup	Butter; softened
1	Cup	Powdered sugar

Instructions:

Combine cake mix, peanut butter, eggs, water and oil in a large bowl; beat on low speed for about 30 seconds. Then on medium speed for 2 minutes.

Fill cupcake liners 2/3 full. Bake at 350 for 18-22 minutes or until toothpick is inserted and comes out clean. Cool completely.

Frosting:

Place chocolate chips in a large bowl. In a small saucepan bring cream just to a boil. Pour over chocolate and whisk until smooth. Cool, stirring occasionally, to room temp. Add butter and powdered sugar; beat until smooth.

Frost cupcakes

Chocolate Mint Wafer

Source: Pat
Origin: US

Type: Cookies
Category: Snack

Quantity	Measure	Item
		Vanilla wafers
		Dark Chocolate Chips
		Peppermint Extract

Instructions:

Melt chocolate and peppermint extract.
Dip vanilla wafer in chocolate; let excess drop off.
Put on wax paper until cooled.

Chocolate Royale Cheesecake Squares

Source: Kappa House	**Type:** Cakes	
Origin: US	**Category:** Dessert	

Quantity	Measure	Item
24		Oreo Cookies (crushed about 2 cups)
1/4	Cup	Butter
4	Package	8 ounce cream cheese
1	Cup	Sugar
2	Tablespoon	Flour
1	Teaspoon	Vanilla
1	Package	8 squares semi-sweet baking chocolate; melted in microwave or on stove top
4		Eggs

Instructions:

Preheat oven to 325 F.

Mix cookies crumbs and butter; press firmly into bottom of 13x9 baking dish.

Bake 10 minutes.

Beat: cream cheese, sugar, flour and vanilla in large bowl with electric mixer on medium speed until well blended.

Add melted chocolate, mix well. Add eggs, 1 at a time, mixing on low speed until well blended.

Pour over crust.

Bake 45 - 50 minutes or until center is almost set.

Refrigerate at least 4 hours or overnight.

Cut into squares.

Refrigerator leftovers.

Chuckwagon Chili Mac

Source:	**Type:** Meat	
Origin:	**Category:** Entree	

Quantity	Measure	Item
1	Package	Macaroni and Cheese (17.5 ounce)
1	Pound	Ground Beef
1	Tablespoon	Chili Powder
1	Teaspoon	Cumin
1	14.5 ounce	can Stewed tomatoes, undrained
1	16 oz.	Kidney Beans, drained
1/3	Cup	Sour cream
1/3	Cup	Cheddar cheese; shredded

Instructions:

Prepare mac and cheese as directed on box.
Brown meat with chili powder and cumin in large skillet on medium heat.
Add tomatoes with liquid and the beans; simmer 3 minutes, stirring occasionally.
Top with sour cream and cheese.

Cinnamon Toast

Source: Ainsley Droege	**Type:** Sweet	
Origin:	**Category:** Breakfast	

Quantity	Measure	Item
1	Slice	White Bread
		Butter
1	Teaspoon	Cinnamon
1	Tablespoon	Powdered sugar

Instructions:

Take white bread put it in a toaster.

After it is toasted, butter, and spread it.

Take a teaspoon of cinnamon sprinkle it on.

Take a tablespoon of powdered sugar and sprinkle it on.

And eat!

Colorful Chicken and Rice

Source: Kappa House	**Type:** Poultry	
Origin:	**Category:** Entree	

Quantity	Measure	Item
1	10 3/4 Ounces	Condensed Cream of Chicken soup, undiluted
1	Cup	Sour cream
½	Cup	Cottage cheese
1	3 ounce	Cream cheese; cubed
3	Cup	Cooked chicken
3	Cup	Cooked rice
1 1/2	Cup	Shredded Monterey Jack Cheese
1	Can	Chopped chilies
1	2 1/4 ounces	Sliced black olives, drained
1/8	Teaspoon	Gallic salt
1 1/2	cups	Crushed corn chips
2	Cup	Shredded lettuce
2	Medium	Tomatoes, chopped

Instructions:

In blender combine soup, sour cream, cottage cheese and cream cheese; process until smooth.

In large bowl stir cheeses, chicken, rice, chilies, olives, and garlic salt.

Pour into greased 2 quart dish.

Bake uncovered at 350 for 25-30 minutes.

Just before serving top with corn chips, lettuce and tomatoes.

Colorful Mediterranean Chickpeas

Source: Katie Kampman
Origin:

Type: Vegetable
Category: Salad

Quantity	Measure	Item
2	15 ounce	can Chickpeas (garbanzo beans), rinsed
3/4	Cup	Roasted red peppers; diced
3/4	Cup	Dried, tart, sweetened cherries, roughly chopped
1/2	Cup	Green onions; sliced
1/2	Cup	Parsley; chopped
1	Tablespoon	Olive oil - extra virgin
1	Tablespoon	Sesame Oil

Salt and pepper to taste

Instructions:

Combine all ingredients and serve.

Confetti Spaghetti

Source: Becki
Origin:

Type: Pasta
Category: Entree

Quantity	Measure	Item
12	Ounce	Spaghetti, cooked
2	Pound	Italian sausage or ground beef
1	Green pepper,	chopped
1	Medium	Onion
14.5	Ounce	Diced tomatoes; undrained
8	Ounce	Tomato sauce
1	Teaspoon	Salt
1	Teaspoon	Chili powder
1/2	Teaspoon	Pepper
½	Teaspoon	Garlic powder
1/4	Teaspoon	Cayenne pepper
1	Cup	Shredded Cheese

Instructions:

Brown meat with green pepper and onion until browned, drain.

Stir in tomatoes, tomato sauce and spices.

Add spaghetti. Put in 9 x 13 dish.

Cover and bake at 350 for 30 minutes.

Sprinkle with cheese and bake 5 more minutes uncovered.

Cookies and Cream Pudding

Source: Kappa House		**Type:** Puddings & Custards
Origin: US		**Category:** Dessert

Quantity	Measure	Item
8		**Oreo Cookies**
2	**Cup**	**Cold Milk**
1	**Package**	**Jell-O Vanilla Instant Pudding (4 ounce size)**
3/4	**Cup**	**Thawed cool whip**

Instructions:

Break one cookie into 4 pieces; reserve for garnish.

Crush remaining cookies, set aside.

Pour milk into bowl; add pudding mix; beat until well blended.

Stir in crushed cookies.

Gently stir in 1/2 cup of cool whip. Spoon into 4 dessert bowls.

Top with remaining cool whip.

Variations: for a double chocolate hit, prepare with chocolate pudding mix.

Corn Salad

Source: Kim Craig	**Type:** Dips & Salsas	
Origin:	**Category:** Appetizer	

Description: This makes quite a bit. If you are not serving a big crowd you might want to only put Frito's in half of the salad and save the other half for later. Then you can add more Frito's

Quantity	Measure	Item
		Chili Cheese Fritos
2	**15 ounce**	**can Corn**
1	**Cup**	**Pepper (green, yellow, orange or red)**
1		**Red onion chopped fine**
1	**Cup**	**Mayo**

Instructions:

Drain corn really well (appx 1 hour)

Mix all ingredients

Cracked Peppercorn Dressing

Source: Pat
Origin:

Type: Dressing
Category: Miscellaneous

Description: I use a couple of cloves of fresh garlic

Quantity	Measure	Item
2	Cup	Mayo
1/4	Cup	Water
1/4	Cup	Milk
1/4	Cup	Buttermilk
2	Tablespoon	Parmesan
1	Tablespoon	Pepper
2	Teaspoon	Green onions
1	Teaspoon	Lemon juice
1/2	Teaspoon	Garlic Salt
1	Teaspoon	Garlic powder

Instructions:

Put the last eight ingredients in a food processor.

When well blended, add water and mayo.

Creamed Spinach

Source: Nancy Ziegler	**Type:** Vegetable
Origin: US	**Category:** Side Dish

Quantity	Measure	Item
1	Box	Chopped Spinach - drained well
1	Egg	Beaten
1/4	Cup	Milk
1	Tablespoon	Butter

Instructions:

Cook spinach first per package directions.

Mix together egg and milk.

Add spinach.

Put butter on top.

Bake for 15 minutes at 350.

Creamy French Dressing

Source: Pat
Origin: Unknown

Type: Dressing
Category: Miscellaneous

Quantity	Measure	Item
1	Cup	Ketchup
1/2	Cup	Mayo
3	Tablespoon	Honey
2	Tablespoon	Water
1	Tablespoon	Olive oil
1	Teaspoon	Lemon juice
1/2	Teaspoon	Nutmeg
1/4	Teaspoon	Salt

Instructions:
Mix all ingredients in blender

Creamy Macaroni Salad

Source: Kappa House		**Type:** Pasta & Rice
Origin: US		**Category:** Salad

Quantity	Measure	Item
1/2	Cup	Mayo
2	Tablespoon	Mustard
1/2	Cup	Sour Cream
1/4	Cup	Half and Half
1/2	Teaspoon	Salt
1	Teaspoon	Pepper
1	Cup	Celery chopped
1/4	Cup	Green Pepper, chopped
1/4	Cup	Red Pepper, Chopped
1/3	Cup	Red Onion
8	Ounce	Elbow Macaroni, cooked and drained

Instructions:

Combine mayo, mustard, sour cream, half and half, salt, and pepper until smooth; fold in remaining ingredients.

Chill for at least 2 hours before serving.

Creamy Pasta with Bacon

Source:		**Type:** Pasta
Origin:		**Category:** Entree

Quantity	Measure	Item
1	9 ounce	Refrigerated linguine
1	Medium	Onion
1	Tablespoon	Olive oil
2	Clove	Garlic
2	Tablespoon	Flour
1 1/2	Cup	Heavy whipping cream
3		Eggs; Beaten
8		Bacon strips; cooked and chopped
1/2	Cup	Parmesan cheesed

Instructions:

Cook linguine according to package directions.

Meanwhile in a large skillet, sauté onion in oil until tender.

Add garlic; cook 1 minute longer.

In a small bowl, whisk flour and cream until smooth.

Bring to a boil, stirring constantly.

Reduce heat; cook and stir for 1 minute.

Remove from heat.

Stir a small amount of hot mixture into eggs, return all to pan, stirring constantly.

Bring to a boil; cook and stir 2 minutes longer.

Add drained linguine to pan.

Stir in bacon and cheese; heat through

Creamy Smashed Potatoes

Source: Pat
Origin:

Type: Vegetable
Category: Side Dish

Description: You can add garlic to the potatoes if you like.

Quantity	Measure	Item
1	Pound	Red potatoes
1/4	Cup	Sour cream
1	Cup	Velveeta cheese
1	Stick	Butter

Instructions:

Put potatoes in pot and bring to a boil.

Let simmer for 20 minutes or until tender. Drain.

Melt butter and Velveeta in pan.

Add sour cream.

Stir into potatoes.

Crockpot Oatmeal

Source: Becki Droege
Origin:

Type: Miscellaneous
Category: Breakfast

Description: We have oatmeal every Sunday before church and try different variations all the time
If you don't have steel cut oats you can use regular oats but NOT quick oats.

Quantity	Measure	Item
1	Cup	Steel cut oats
2	Cup	Evaporated milk
2	Cup	Water
1/4	Cup	Brown sugar
1	Tablespoon	Butter
1/2	Teaspoon	Vanilla extract
1	Teaspoon	Cinnamon

Instructions:

Combine all ingredients in a crock-pot

Cook on low for 8 hrs

It is best to use a bowl in your crock-pot with water around it like a double broiler because it really gets caked on otherwise

Variations: instead of vanilla use banana extract and serve with banana and almonds
instead of brown sugar & cinnamon use peanut butter and honey
add 1 cup of raisins or some dried fruit
top with fresh fruit
add butter or jam or honey

Dulce de Leche Cheesecake

Source: Kappa House		**Type:** Cakes
Origin: Mexico		**Category:** Dessert

Quantity	Measure	Item
3	8 ounce	Package Cream Cheese
1/2	Cup	Sugar
1	Cup	Mexican caramel spread (dulce de leche)
1/2	Cup	Sour Cream
3		Eggs
1	Cup	Honey multi-grain cereal flakes with oat clusters
1/2	Cup	Cool-Whip

Instructions:

Heat oven to 350.

Beat cream cheese and 1/4 cup sugar until well blended.

Add caramel spread and sour cream; mix well.

Add eggs, 1 at a time, mixing on low speed until blended.

Pour into 9" spring form pan.

Bake 50-55 minutes.

Run a knife or metal spatula around rim of pan to loosen cheesecake; cool before removing rim.

Refrigerate 4 hours.

Meanwhile cook remaining sugar in saucepan until melted and brown.

Remove from heat.

Stir in crushed cereal; spread into thin layer in shallow pan.

Cool.

Top cheese cake with Cool Whip and cereal just before serving.

Dutch Babies

Source: Becki Droege
Origin:

Type: Miscellaneous
Category: Dessert

Description: This recipe came from a recipe swap on a road trip to Springfield, IL. Rachelle said it was one of her family favorites.

Quantity	Measure	Item
5		Egg
1/2	Cup	Butter
1 1/4	Cup	Milk
1 1/4	Cup	Flour

Instructions:

Turn oven to 450.
Melt butter; mix eggs, milk, and flour until fluffy.
Pour batter into butter and cook for 20 minutes.
Top with powdered sugar or syrup.

Easy Cheesy Potatoes

Source:	Type: Vegetable
Origin:	Category: Side Dish

Quantity	Measure	Item
1	Pound	Frozen diced hash browns potatoes
1	Can	Cream of chicken soup
16	Ounce	Sour Cream
12	Ounce	Shredded sharp cheddar cheese
1/2	Cup	Onion
1	Stick	Butter
1	Teaspoon	Salt
1/2	Teaspoon	Pepper

Instructions:

Mix all ingredients.

Pour into greased 9 x 13 pan.

Bake at 350 for 1 hour.

Escalloped Corn

Source: Grandma Burger
Origin: US

Type: Vegetable
Category: Side Dish

Description: This is my grandmother's recipe and she baked this in a quick oven. I'd say that is 375-400. The cheese will melt and will turn a golden brown.

Quantity	Measure	Item
1	Can	Corn
1/2	Cup	Cracker crumbs
4	Tablespoon	Grated Cheese
2/3	Cup	Milk
1		Egg
		Salt and pepper to taste
2	Tablespoon	Butter

Instructions:

Mix thoroughly and bake for 35 minutes in quick oven (375).

Farm House Chicken Dinner

Source:	**Type:** Meat
Origin:	**Category:** Entree

Quantity	Measure	Item
1/4	Cup	Flour
1/2	Teaspoon	Pepper
4	Small	Chicken breasts, skin removed
1/4	Cup	Zesty Italian dressing
2	Cup	Baby carrots
1	Medium	Onion, cut in wedges
1	14.5 ounce can	Chicken broth
2	Cup	Brown rice - uncooked
4	Ounce	Cream cheese
2	Tablespoon	Parsley

Instructions:

Mix flour and pepper in shallow dish.

Add chicken, coat evenly both sides.

Heat dressing in skillet, add chicken.

Cook until golden brown on one side (5-6 minutes).

Turn chicken over; add carrots, onion wedges, and 1 cup of broth.

Cover and reduce heat to medium-low and cook for 20 minutes or until chicken and carrots are tender.

Prepare rice as directed on package.

Put in serving dish.

Spoon chicken and vegetable over rice (use slotted spoon so as not to take the juice).

Add cheese and remaining broth to skillet, increase heat to high.

Cook until cheese is melted and sauce is well blended; stirring constantly,

Spoon over chicken and rice, sprinkle with parsley.

Fiesta Taco Casserole

Source:		**Type:** Meat
Origin: Mexico		**Category:** Entree

Quantity	Measure	Item
1	Pound	Ground Beef
1	15-16 ounce can	Spicy chili beans in sauce; undrained
1	Cup	Chunky Salsa
2	Cup	Broken Tortilla Chips
3/4	Cup	Sour Cream
4		Green Onions
1		Tomato chopped
1	Cup	Cheddar Cheese
		Lettuce if desired
		Additional Salsa if desired

Instructions:

Brown ground beef and drain.

Stir in salsa and beans.

Heat to boiling; stirring occasionally.

In greased 2 quart casserole, place broken tortilla chips.

Top with beef mixture, spread with sour cream on top

Sprinkle with onion, tomato and cheese.

Bake uncovered for 20-30 minute at 350 until hot and bubbly.

Serve with lettuce and additional salsa.

Variations: Substitute ground turkey instead of ground beef.

Four Berry Spinach Salad

Source: Kappa House		**Type:** Fruit
Origin:		**Category:** Salad

Quantity	Measure	Item
1	Tablespoon	Canola oil
1	Tablespoon	Orange Juice
1	Tablespoon	Red wine vinegar
1	Tablespoon	Balsamic vinegar
1	Tablespoon	Water
2	Teaspoon	Lemon juice
1/2	Teaspoon	Sugar
1/2	Teaspoon	Poppy Seeds
1/8	Teaspoon	Ground all spice
		Dash Cinnamon
4	Cup	Each raspberries, blueberries, blackberries, and sliced strawberries
2	Teaspoon	Walnuts; chopped and toasted
1		Bowl Spinach leaf

Instructions:

For dressing mix the first 10 ingredients in a jar and shake well.

Combine spinach and berries.

Drizzle with dressing and sprinkle with walnuts.

Four Cheese Baked Ziti

Source:	**Type:** Meat	
Origin:	**Category:** Entree	

Quantity	Measure	Item
1	16 ounce pkg	Ziti or small tube pasta
2	10 ounce	Alfredo Sauce
1	Cup	Sour cream
2		Eggs; beaten slightly
1	15 ounce carton	Ricotta cheese
1/2	Cup	Parmesan Cheese
1/4	Cup	Romano cheese
1/4	Cup	Parsley; minced
1 1/4	Cup	Mozzarella cheese;

Instructions:

Cook ziti according to package directions; drain and return to pan.

Stir in Alfredo sauce and sour cream; spoon half into a lightly greased 3 quart dish.

In small bowl, combine eggs, ricotta cheese, 1/4 cup parmesan cheese, Ramona Cheese and parsley; spread over pasta. Top with remaining pasta mixture; sprinkle with mozzarella cheese and remaining parmesan cheese

Cover and bake at 350 for 25 minutes. Uncover and bake another 5-10 minutes longer or until bubbly.

Four Cheese Bow Ties

Source: Kappa House		**Type:** Pasta
Origin:		**Category:** Entree

Quantity	Measure	Item
1	16 oz.	Bow Tie Pasta
2	14.5 oz	Diced tomato
1/4	Cup	Butter
1/4	Cup	Flour
1/4	Teaspoon	Salt
1/4	Teaspoon	Pepper
1 1/2	Cup	Milk
1 1/2	Cup	Mozzarella cheese
1 1/3	Cup	Romano cheese
1/2	Cup	Shredded parmesan cheese
1/4	Cup	Blue cheese
1/2	Cup	Fresh parsley

Instructions:

Cook pasta according to package directions.

Meanwhile, drain tomatoes, reserving 1 1/4 cup juice; set aside.

In large saucepan, melt butter, stir in flour, salt, and pepper until smooth; gradually add milk and reserved tomato juice.

Bring to a boil. cook and stir for 2 minutes or until thicken.

Remove from heat.

Add tomatoes, pasta and sauce.

Stir in Cheeses and parsley.

Transfer to greased 3 qt baking dish.

Bake uncovered at 375 for 30-35 minutes or until bubbly.

French Onion Soup

Source: Kappa House
Origin:

Type: Miscellaneous
Category: Soup

Description: This recipe is for individual crocks of soup. If serving a large crowd, you can put the soup in a crockpot. Then let your guests assemble their own soup in a bowl.

Quantity	Measure	Item
		Provolone Cheese
		Salt & Pepper
5-6		Sweet onions
2	Can	Beef Broth
1	Cube	Beef Bouillon
		Texas Toast
1	Tablespoon	Butter

Instructions:

Melt butter in skillet and sauté onions until golden brown. in sauce pan add onions, beef broth and beef bouillon.

Simmer about 20 minutes.

Cook toast according to package.

Once soup has simmered, add to crock.

Cut toast in pieces and place on top and submerge into soup in crock.

Cover with provolone cheese and bake in oven for 5-7 minutes until cheese is golden brown.

French Toast Strata

Source: Becki
Origin:

Type: Miscellaneous
Category: Breakfast

Quantity	Measure	Item
1	Pound	Cinnamon bread, cubed
1	8 oz. pkg	Cream cheese, cubed
8		Eggs
2 1/2	Cup	Milk
6	Tablespoon	Butter; divided
1/4	Cup	Maple syrup

Instructions:

Arrange half of the bread cubes in a greased 9 x 13 baking dish.

Top with cream cheese and rest of bread. In blender combine eggs, milk, butter and maple syrup; process until smooth.

Pour over bread.

Cover and refrigerate overnight.

Remove from fridge 30 minutes before baking.

Bake uncovered at 350 for 35-40 minutes.

Let stand 10 minutes before serving.

Frisch's Pizza

Source: Becki Droege		**Type:** Meat
Origin:		**Category:** Entree

Description : A good friend of mine gave me this recipe and it is soo good (plus it is very easy to make). I knew mom would love it because she is a Frisch fan. Thanx Brandy:)

Quantity	Measure	Item
		Lettuce
1		Boboli Pizza Crust
1	Pound	Ground beef/sirloin; browned
		Sharp cheddar cheese the desired amount for your family
		Pickles
1	Small Jar	Frisch's tartar sauce

Instructions:

Spread tartar sauce on pizza crust.

Spread beef on top.

Sprinkle pickles; top with cheese.

Bake at 350 until cheese melts.

Put lettuce on top.

Cut and serve.

Frito Candy

Source: Becki Schilling Droege
Origin:

Type: Candy
Category: Dessert

Description: My dear friend Mitzi brought this to so many crops and I could not stop eating it. I never wanted to recipe because it was just too good, so when I "accidently" got it and realized how simple it was I was totally doomed! You cannot eat just one and can make more in no time at all:)

Quantity	Measure	Item
1	Cup	Light Karo Syrup
1	Cup	Sugar
1	Cup	Peanut butter
1		Bag Fritos

Instructions:

Lay frito out on a baking sheet with sides.
Bring karo and sugar to a boil.
Add peanut butter
Pour over fritos.
Cool and cut.

Frozen Virgin Margaritas

Source: Kappa House
Origin:

Type: Miscellaneous
Category: Beverage

Quantity	Measure	Item
2	Tablespoon	Kosher salt
1/2		Lime, cut into 4 wedges
1	6 ounce	can Frozen limeade concentrate, thawed
1/4	Cup	Orange juice
4	Cup	Ice cubes

Instructions:

Place salt in a shallow dish.

Rub the rim of each of 4 margarita glasses with a lime wedge and dip the rims into the salt; set the lime wedges aside.

In blender, blend the limeade, orange juice, and ice cubes on high speed for 1 - 2 minutes, or until well blended and the ice cubes are crushed.

Pour evenly into the glasses and garnish with lime wedges.

Fruit Cooler

Source: Pat	**Type:** Fruit
Origin: US	**Category:** Beverage

Quantity	Measure	Item
2	Cup	Orange juice
1	Cup	Pineapple juice
1 1/2	Cup	Strawberries - fresh
1/4	Cup	Powdered sugar
1	Cup	Chilled carbonated water

Instructions:

Put first four ingredients in blender.

Add carbonated water and serve over ice.

Fruit Salad with Poppy Seed Dressing

Source: Kappa House	**Type:** Fruit	
Origin: Unknown	**Category:** Salad	

Quantity	Measure	Item
2	Cup	Pineapple
2	Cup	Grapes
2	Medium	Bananas, sliced
2	Cup	Fresh Strawberries
1/3	Cup	Red Wine Vinegar
3/4	Cup	Sugar
1	Teaspoon	Ground Mustard
3/4	Teaspoon	Salt
3/4	Cup	Vegetable oil
1	Tablespoon	Poppy Seeds

Instructions:

In blender or food processor, combine the vinegar, sugar, mustard, and salt.

Gradually add oil.

Stir in poppy seeds.

Just before serving combine fruit.

Pour on Dressing.

Fusille with Spicy Pasta

Source: Katy Freeman - Kappa
Origin:

Type: Pasta
Category: Entree

Quantity	Measure	Item
1	Cup	Chopped walnuts
2	Clove	Garlic
1	Jalapeno pepper,	chopped
2	Cup	Asago cheese - grated
2	Teaspoon	Salt
1	Teaspoon	Pepper
2	Cup	Baby spinach
3	Cup	Arugula
1/4	Cup	Olive oil
1	Pound	Fusille

Instructions:

In food processor or blender, combine walnuts, garlic, jalapeno, grated cheese, salt and pepper.

Process until smooth.

Add spinach and arugula, and process until blended.

Add the oil gradually until mixed.

Cook fusille according to package directions - reserving 1/3 cup of the hot water.

Add the hot water to the pesto to thin and then combine pesto and pasta.

Garnish with a little asiago cheese and serve

Variations: Put some crushed red pepper flakes on the pasta before adding pesto for an extra kick.

Garlic Butter Shrimp

Source: Pat	**Type:** Seafood	
Origin: US	**Category:** Entree	

Quantity	Measure	Item
1	Pound	Shrimp
3	Cloves	Garlic
1/4	Cup	Butter
3	Tablespoon	Lemon Juice

Instructions:

Sauté first 3 ingredients for 5 minutes.

Add lemon juice.

Serve over rice.

Garlic Snacks

Source: Ellen Dodd
Origin:

Type: Miscellaneous
Category: Snack

Quantity	Measure	Item
1	17.5 ounce box	Rice Chex
1	17.5 ounce box	Corn Chex
1	16 ounce box	Wheat Chex
1	7 ounce box	Cheerios
1	16 ounce box	Pretzel Sticks
1	Pound	Mixed Nuts
5	sticks	Butter + 3 tablespoon
1 1/2	Teaspoon	Celery Seed
1 1/2	Teaspoon	Onion powder
2	Teaspoon	Worcestershire
5-6	Teaspoon	Garlic Powder

Instructions:

Melt butter in saucepan.

When melted add seasonings.

Stir thoroughly.

Layer cereals & pretzels in a large turkey roaster,.

Pour butter mixture over dry ingredients.

Stir to mix.

Bake at 250 for 2 hours; stirring every 15 minutes.

Add nuts the last 45 minutes.

German Potato Salad

Source: Grandma Burger **Origin:** German		**Type:** Vegetable **Category:** Salad

Description: Grandma Burger rarely bothered with a recipe. She just wrote the ingredients down on paper. You have to figure out the rest. On this recipe, when it says vinegar, I'm pretty sure that it means apple cider. However, they make so many types of vinegar now that it would to fun to try other types.

Quantity	Measure	Item
2	Quarts	Boiled Potatoes
1	Teaspoon	Salt
1/2	Teaspoon	Pepper
3	Small	Onions minced
1/2	Pound	Bacon
1/2	Cup	Vinegar
3	Tablespoon	Sugar

Instructions:

Fry bacon and crumble.

Sauce onions and add vinegar, sugar and remaining seasonings.

Bring to a boil and pour over potatoes.

Mix well.

Can be garnish with parsley and hard boiled eggs.

Glazed Pecans

Source: Ellen Dogg
Origin:

Type: Miscellaneous
Category: Snack

Quantity	Measure	Item
1/4	Cup	Butter
1/4	Cup	Light corn syrup
2	Tablespoon	Water
1	Teaspoon	Salt
1	Pound	Pecan halves

Instructions:

Preheat oven to 250.

Line a baking sheet with foil.

Combine butter, corn syrup, water and salt in a small saucepan.

Bring to a boil.

Stir in pecans and mix well to coat pecans on all sides.

Spread evenly on baking sheet and bake for 40 minutes; stirring every 10 minutes.

Grape Salad

Source: Ella Mae Perfect
Origin:

Type: Fruit
Category: Salad

Description : I like to make the pecan caramelized. Just put granulated sugar in a pan. When it is melted, add pecans. Spread on non stick cookie sheet. when cooled, break apart and add to grapes.

Quantity	Measure	Item
		Green Seedless Grapes
		Red Seedless Grapes
		Pecans pieces
1	Cup	Sugar
1	Cup	Sour Cream
1	8 ounce	Cream Cheese

Instructions:

After washing grapes, make sure they are really dry.

Put grapes and pecans in a large bowl.

Mix the sugar, sour cream and cream cheese.

Pour over grapes and stir until coated.

Refrigerated for an hour or so before serving.

Greek Salad

Source: Kappa House
Origin:

Type: First Course
Category: Salad

Quantity	Measure	Item
1	Large	Cucumber, chopped
2		Roma tomatoes, chopped
1	5 ounce	Pitted Kalama Olives
1	4 ounce	Feta Cheese, crumbled
1		Red Onion, halved and thinly sliced
10	Ounce	Romaine Lettuce
10	Ounce	Baby Greens

Instructions:

Add chopped cucumber, chopped tomatoes, Kalama olives, feta cheese, red onion, romaine lettuce and baby greens to large serving bowl.

Top with vinaigrette dressing.

Green Beans

Source: Kappa House   **Type:** Vegetable
Origin: US   **Category:** Side Dish

Description: I realize there are no amounts with these ingredients. I use a large skittel and coat with olive oil. Put in the frozen green beans and add the rest of the ingredients to taste.

Quantity	Measure	Item
		Frozen Green Beans
		Gallic Powder
		Onion Powder
		Salt
		Pepper
		Olive Oil

Instructions:

Cover the bottom of a skillet with olive oil.

Put in frozen green beans.

Generously sprinkle with garlic and onion powder.

Add pepper and salt to taste.

Turn the green beans until they are no longer frozen and hot.

Simple yet delicious.

Green Beans With Colored Peppers

Source: Kappa House	**Type:** Vegetable
Origin:	**Category:** Side Dish

Quantity	Measure	Item
1	22 ounce	bag Green beans
1	Tablespoon	Lemon Juice
2	Teaspoon	Dijon Mustard
1	Tablespoon	Fresh Basil or 1 teaspoon dried
2	Teaspoon	Fresh Thyme or 3/4 teaspoon dried
1	Tablespoon	Olive oil
1		Red bell pepper; cut into strips
1		Yellow bell pepper; cut into strips
1/2	Teaspoon	Salt

Instructions:

In a 12" skillet cook green beans & pepper until tender (around 8-10 minutes).

In a small bowl combine lemon juice, mustard, basil, and thyme.

Add to vegetables.

Add salt and pepper as desired.

Serve warm.

Grilled Beef and Provolone Sandwiches

Source: Pat	**Type:** Meat	
Origin:	**Category:** Sandwich	

Quantity	Measure	Item
4	slices	Vienna or Italian bread
2	Tablespoon	Basil pesto
1/4	Pound	Thinly sliced deli roast beef
1/4	Cup	Thin slices roasted red bell peppers
2	slices	Provolone
1	Tablespoon	Butter

Instructions:

Heat Grill or sandwich maker.

Spread one side of each slice of bread with pesto. On 2 slices of the bread, layer beef, roasted peppers and cheese. Top with remaining slices of bread, pesto side down. Brush outside of sandwiches with butter.

Grill 3 or 5 minutes or until bread is toasted and cheese melts.

Guacamole - Quickly

Source: Kappa House	**Type:** Dips & Salsas	
Origin:	**Category:** Sauces	

Quantity	Measure	Item
3		Red pepper flakes; optional per taste Avocados; halved, seeded, peeled, and smashed
2	1 ounce	Packets Great Guacamole powder
3	Tablespoon	Mayo

Instructions:

Mix dry packets with avocados.

Mix well, then add mayo and blend well.

Guacamole - Scratch

Source: Kappa House	**Type:** Dips & Salsas
Origin:	**Category:** Sauces

Quantity	Measure	Item
3		Avocadoes; halved seeded, peeled, and smashed
1		Lime; juiced
1/2	Teaspoon	Kosher salt
1/2	Teaspoon	Cumin
1/4	Teaspoon	Cayenne
1/4	Teaspoon	Red pepper flakes
1/2	Medium	Onion; diced
1	Tablespoon	Cilantro
1	Clove	Garlic
2	Tablespoon	Salsa
2	Tablespoon	Mayo

Instructions:

In a large bowl place the avocado pulp and lime juice, toss to coat.

Mix in the remaining ingredients and blend well.

Let stand for an hour at room temperature before serving.

Guacamole Hummus

Source: Kappa House
Origin: Mexico

Type: Dips & Salsas
Category: Appetizer

Quantity	Measure	Item
1	Can	Chickpeas; drained and rinsed
1	Bunch	Cilantro; washed and dried
1	Clove	Garlic
1		Avocado
3	Tablespoon	Olive oil
1	Teaspoon	Lemon
1	Teaspoon	Water

Instructions:

In food processor, combine chickpeas, cilantro, garlic and avocado.

Process until finely chopped.

Add olive oil in a slow and steady stream.

Add lemon and water.

Mix until smooth.

Season to taste with coarse salt and pepper.

serve with tortilla chips.

Gypsy Goulash

Source: Grandma Burger	**Type:** Meat
Origin:	**Category:** Side Dish

Description: This recipe tickles me because it was made before air conditioning. The recipe says to prepare the dish in the cool of the morning, reheating it in the late afternoon over the back-yard fire or the canned heat stove. Since there were no microwaves; it is suggested to reheat by placing the casserole in a heavy pan containing hot water.

Quantity	Measure	Item
1/2	Pound	Bacon
3		Green peppers
1		Onion
2	Can	Red Kidney Beans
1	Quart	Can tomato

Instructions:

Fry bacon and set aside.

Sautee green peppers and onion.

Add kidney beans and tomatoes.

Cook for 2 or 3 minutes.

Stir well and place in casserole dish.

Cover and cook one hour in a moderate oven (350).

Remove from oven and sprinkle with grated cheese and bacon.

Return to oven and cook until cheese is melted.

Ham and Cheese Omelet Roll

Source: Becki Schilling Droege	**Type:** Egg Dish
Origin:	**Category:** Breakfast

Quantity	Measure	Item
4	Ounce	Cream cheese; softened
3/4	Cup	Milk
2	Tablespoon	All purpose flour
¼	Teaspoon	Salt
12		Eggs
2	Tablespoon	Dijon mustard
2 1/4	Cup	Cheddar cheese; shredded & divided
2	Cup	Cubed ham
1/2	Cup	Green onions; chopped

Instructions:

Line jelly roll pan with parchment paper, grease paper.

Mix cream cheese and milk, add flour and salt.

In separate bowl, beat eggs until well blended. add cream cheese and mix well.

Pour into pan.

Bake at 375 for 35 minutes - until eggs are puffy and set.

Spread with mustard.

Sprinkle with 1 cup of cheese, ham, onion, and the other cup of cheese.

Roll from short side peeling paper away.

Sprinkle remaining cheese on top.

Bake 5 more minutes until cheese melts.

Hamburger Pie

Source: Ellen Dodd
Origin:

Type: Meat
Category: Entree

Quantity	Measure	Item
		Oregano to taste
		Salt and Pepper to taste
		Garlic Powder to taste
		Worcestershire sauce to taste
		Mashed potatoes
1.5	Pound	Ground Beef
1	Can	Tomato Soup
1	Medium	Onion chopped
1	15 ounce	can Green Beans

Instructions:

Brown Beef and onion.

Mix in green beans, soup and seasonings.

Put in casserole.

Prepare mashed potatoes.

Spread potatoes on top of meat mixture.

Bake 1/2 - 3/4 hours at 350.

Iced Nuts

Source: Ellen Dodd   **Type:** Miscellaneous
Origin: **Category:** Snack

Quantity	Measure	Item
1 1/2	Cup	Blanched whole almonds, pecan halves, walnut halves and/or cashews
1/2	Cup	Sugar
2	Tablespoon	Butter
1/2	Teaspoon	Vanilla

Instructions:

Line a baking sheet with foil.

Butter the foil and set aside.

Combine nuts, sugar and butter in a skillet.

Cook over medium heat, carefully stirring constantly about 9 minutes or until sugar melts and turns

a rich brown color.

Remove heat.

Immediately stir in vanilla.

Spread nuts on the prepared baking sheet.

Cool completely.

Break into clusters.

Store tightly covered.

Italian Pasta Bake

Source: Kappa House
Origin: Italy

Type: Pasta
Category: Entree

Quantity	Measure	Item
		Mushroom to taste
		Mozzarella Cheese to top
1 1/2	**Cup**	**Uncooked Penne Pasta**
1/2	**Pound**	**Italian Sausage**
1		**Onion**
1		**Small Zucchini**
14 1/2	**Ounce**	**Diced tomatoes with basil, garlic and Oregano**
15	**Ounce**	**Tomato sauce**

Instructions:

Cook penne pasta per package directions.

Brown sausage (drain fat), add onion, zucchini, mushrooms, and tomatoes.

Simmer for 20 minutes.

You can either mix in pasta or serve over top.

Add shredded mozzarella cheese to top.

Italian Spaghetti

Source: Grandma Burger
Origin: Italy

Type: Pasta
Category: Entree

Description: This recipe was my maternal grandmother's recipe. She was born in 1886 (yes really). So, when she developed this recipe it was in the early 1900's. I have the recipe exactly as she wrote and then added the present day amounts. Her directions were a little different also. I will give you her advice: Boil spaghetti in salted water 10 minutes, then drain, pour cold water over, let drain again. Have onion cut fine and with 10 cents worth ground beef, browned slightly in skillet, then add tomatoes, 1/2 cheese, salt, pepper garlic and bring to boil. Let cook slowly one hour on top of stove only stirring to keep from sticking. 1/2 bottle of catsup is desired. Sprinkle with 5 cents worth of cheese.

Quantity	Measure	Item
		Catsup can be added if desired
10	**Cents**	**Ground Beef (1 pound)**
1	**Pound**	**Uncooked Spaghetti**
1		**Onion cut fine**
		Salt to taste
		Pepper to taste
1	**14 1/2 ounce**	**Can Tomato**
1		**Garlic clove**
5		**Cents Cheese (1 - 2 cups as desired)**

Instructions:

Cook spaghetti per package directions.
Brown ground beef with onion, salt, pepper, garlic, add tomatoes and half of cheese.
When done spread over spaghetti and sprinkle with rest of cheese.

Variations: Can add bacon, sausage, mushrooms, peppers if desired.

Lasagna Mexican

Source: Kappa House
Origin: Mexico

Type: Meat
Category: Entree

Description: Can be made with Chicken also.

Quantity	Measure	Item
		Flour tortillas
		Lettuce
		Sour cream
		Salsa
		Tomatoes
		Taco chips
		Cheese sauce
1 1/2	Pound	Ground beef
1/2	Cup	Onions; chopped
1		Package Taco seasoning
1	Can	Refried beans
1	Can	Green chilies
2	Cup	Cheddar cheese

Instructions:

Brown beef with onions.

Stir in taco sauce, beans, and chilies.

Spread small amount of mixture in bottom of baking dish.

Cover with layer of tortillas (I tear the tortillas into bite size pieces).

Spread half of remaining meat mixture over tortillas, sprinkle with cheese

Cover with another layer of tortillas.

Spread remaining meat mixture over tortillas and sprinkle with remaining cheese.

Cover and Bake at 350 until hot.

Serve over chopped lettuce, sour cream, salsa, tomatoes and taco chips.

Pour cheese sauce on top.

Layered Nacho Dip

Source: Pat	**Type**: Meat	
Origin: US	**Category**: Appetizer	

Classification: Beef

Quantity	Measure	Item
		Tortilla chips
1	**Pound**	**Lean ground beef**
1	**Medium**	**Onion, finely chopped**
1	**Can**	**Chopped green chilies (4 ounces)**
1	**Can**	**Refried beans (16 ounces)**
2	**Cup**	**Cheddar cheese, shredded**
3/4	**Cup**	**Thick taco sauce**
1	**Cup**	**Sour cream**
1/4	**Cup**	**Green onion, chopped**
1/4	**Cup**	**Black olives, chopped**

Instructions:

Preheat oven to 400 degrees F.

Crumble and brown ground beef in skillet with onion for 8 to 10 minutes, or until beef is no longer pink. Drain fat and rinse, if desired.

Spread beans in thin layer in 9-inch x 13-inch baking dish. Combine beef, onion and chilies and place on bean layer. Drizzle with taco sauce.

Bake, uncovered for 20 minutes.

Top with grated cheese, dollop with sour cream, and sprinkle with green onions and black olives.

Serve hot as a dip with plenty of taco chips.

Lemon Bars

Source: Claire Stegman - Kappa   **Type:** Cakes
Origin: **Category:** Dessert

Quantity	Measure	Item
1	Cup	Butter
¼	Teaspoon	Salt
2 1/4	Cup	Flour
1/2	Cup	Powdered sugar
1		Zest of Lemon
6	Tablespoon	Lemon
4		Eggs
2	Cup	Sugar

Instructions:

Preheat oven to 350.

Mix butter, salt, 2 cups flour and powdered sugar.

Press firmly into a 9 x 13 pan.

Bake 15-20 minutes until golden brown at edges.

Gradually add sugar, grated lemon zest and lemon juice to beaten eggs.

Sift remaining 1/4 cup flour and fold into gently.

Pour over slightly cooled crust.

Return to oven and bake 20-25 minutes longer.

Remove from oven.

Sprinkle with powdered sugar.

Cool and cut into bars.

Macaroni Chicken Dinner

Source: Becki Schilling Droege	**Type:** Pasta
Origin:	**Category:** Entree

Description: The chicken can be made in the crock pot or pressure cooker which makes it so tender. It will just fall apart when you take it out. If you put the chicken in the crock pot, you can let it cook all night.

Quantity	Measure	Item
2	pounds	Cooked chicken
1		Cream of mushroom or chicken soup
1	Cup	Milk
1/2	Cup	Half & half
2	Cup	Macaroni; uncooked
8	Ounce	Cheddar cheese
2		Celery ribs; chopped
4		Hardboiled eggs
3/4	Cup	Garlic flavored bread crumbs
2-3	Tablespoon	Butter

Instructions:

Combine the soup, broth, milk and half & half.

Stir in chicken, macaroni, cheese, celery and eggs.

Place in a greased 3 quart casserole.

Cover and bake for 30 minutes at 350.

Combine bread crumbs and butter and sprinkle over top.

Return to oven for 20 minutes or until macaroni is tender.

Let stand for 5 minutes before serving.

Mac & Cheese

Source: Ellen Dodd		**Type:** Pasta
Origin:		**Category:** Side Dish

Quantity	Measure	Item
8	Ounce	Uncooked macaroni
8	Ounce	Ragu double cheddar cheese sauce
2	Tablespoon	Butter; cut into pieces
8	Ounce	Shredded cheddar cheese
1 1/2	Cup	Milk

Instructions:

Preheat oven to 375.

Cook macaroni per package directions.

Spoon Cheese sauce into large bowl and add butter.

Drain macaroni well and pour into bowl with cheese sauce while still hot.

Stir until well coated.

Add Shredded cheddar and continue to stir until butter melts.

Add milk and stir until well blended.

Pour into casserole.

Bake 30 to 35 minutes until top begins to brown.

Mango Tango Salsa

Source: Kappa House   **Type:** Dips & Salsas
Origin: **Category:** Sauces

Quantity	Measure	Item
3	Large	Mangos, peeled, pitted and diced
1		Medium Jalapenos Pepper, stemmed, seeded and minced
2/3	Cup	Red bell pepper; diced
1/3	Cup	Onion; diced
2	Tablespoon	Fresh cilantro; chopped
2	Tablespoon	Lime juice
1	Tablespoon	Olive Oil
1/2	Teaspoon	Ground cumin
1/2	Teaspoon	Kosher Salt

Instructions:

Stir all ingredients in a medium bowl

Meatball Dunkers

Source: Becki Droege	**Type:** Meat
Origin:	**Category:** Entree

Description: These are super easy and my kids just scarf them up :)

Quantity	Measure	Item
1		Bag Pre-cooked frozen meatballs
2	cans	Crescent roll dough
1	Jar	Pasta sauce

Instructions:

Thaw meatballs

Roll out crescent rolls and cut (make 3 meatballs for each strip of crescent)

Wrap dough around meatballs

Bake according to dough instructions

Serve with pasta sauce for dipping.

Mexicali Cornbread Casserole

Source: Becki Droege	**Type:** Meat	
Origin: Mexico	**Category:** Entree	

Quantity	Measure	Item
		Sour cream
2 1/2	cups	Corn
1	lb	Ground beef
1	pkg	Taco seasoning
1	Box	Jiffy cornmeal
2	Cup	Milk
3		Eggs
		Salt
		Pepper
2	Cup	Taco-flavored cheese

Instructions:

Preheat oven to 375

Brown ground beef and add taco seasoning according to directions

Mix jiffy with the taco meat

put in 9x13 casserole

Combine lightly beaten eggs with milk, salt & pepper

Pour over taco meat

Bake covered for 45 minutes

Top with cheese and bake uncovered until cheese is melted

Serve with sour cream

Mexican Casserole Made Easy

Source: Becki Droege	**Type:** Meat
Origin:	**Category:** Entree

Quantity	Measure	Item
1	Can	Beans - your choice
1	Can	Rotel
1	Cup	Salsa
1/2	Can	Cream of mushroom soup
1/4-1/2	Cup	Sour Cream
1	Pound	Ground beef
1/2		onion Diced
		Seasoning as desired: chili powder, garlic powder, salt, pepper
1	Cup	Grated cheese
		Tortilla chips
2	Cup	Cooked rice

Instructions:

Sauté onion and add meat to brown; drain.

Add all 11 ingredients except cheese.

Spread rice in bottom of 9 x 13 pan; pour meat over top; sprinkle with cheese.

Cook for 30 minutes at 350 or until hot and bubbly.

Serve with tortillas, extra salsa, and sour cream

Mock Turtle Soup

Source: Audrey Schemenaur	**Type:** Meat	
Origin:	**Category:** Soup	

Quantity	Measure	Item
2	Quart	Water
1	Pound	Ground Beef
1	15 ounce	bottle Ketchup
1/3	Cup	Worcestershire
1	Large	Onion
2	Tablespoon	lemon juice
1	Tablespoon	Salt
		Dash pepper
1	Ketchup bottle	full of water
26		Gingersnaps, rolled fine
2		Hard boiled eggs, chopped fine

Instructions:

Combine first 8 ingredients.

Break meat up fine

Simmer 1 1/2 hours

Add water to gingersnaps. Stir and blend until smooth.

Add to first mixture and simmer 1/2 hour longer; stirring occasionally

Add chopped eggs a few minutes before serving.

Freezes well.

Old Fashioned Turkey Soup

Source: Kappa House	**Type:** Meat
Origin:	**Category:** Soup

Description: Can use wild rice also. If you prefer barley instead of rice - omit rice and stewed tomatoes and add 1 cup of barley.

Quantity	Measure	Item
5	Cup	Chicken Broth
3	Cup	Cubed Turkey
1	28 ounce can	Stewed tomatoes
1	Large	Onion; diced
2	Large	Carrots; shredded
1	Cup	Celery; diced
1	10 ounce	Spinach; thawed
3/4	Cup	Peas
3/4	Cup	Brown rice
4	cubes	Bouillon
2	Teaspoon	Salt
3/4	Teaspoon	Pepper
1/2	Teaspoon	Marjoram
1/2	Teaspoon	Thyme

Instructions:

Put all the ingredients in a large pot and bring to a boil.

Reduce heat; cover and simmer for 30 minutes or until rice and veggies are tender.

Pasta Salad

Source:	**Type:** Pasta	
Origin:	**Category:** Salad	

Quantity	Measure	Item
		Grated Parmesan Cheese to taste
1	Pound	Rainbow rotini (cooked according to package directions and cooled.
1	8 ounce	Wishbone Italian Dressing
1	Package	Good Seasons Dry Italian Seasoning (dressing mix)
1		Tomato; diced
1		Green pepper; diced
1	4 ounce	Can sliced black olives
1/2		Large package pepperoni; cut into strips

Instructions:

Combine all ingredients and refrigerator overnight.

Pasta with Fresh Tomatoes; Basil and Chicken

Source: Kappa House	**Type:** Meat
Origin: US	**Category:** Entree

Quantity	Measure	Item
6		Boneless, Skinless Chicken Breasts halved (cut into bite size pieces)
3		Ripe tomato
2		Garlic Clove
2	Tablespoon	Fresh parsley; chopped
2	Tablespoon	Fresh basil; chopped
1/2	Teaspoon	Sugar
1/2	Teaspoon	Salt
1/4	Teaspoon	Pepper
2	Tablespoon	Lemon Juice
1	Tablespoon	Olive Oil
6-8	Ounce	Uncooked linguini
1/4	Cup	Parmesan Cheese; shredded

Instructions:

Season chicken on both sides with salt and pepper. In a large skillet heat 1 1/2 teaspoon olive oil over medium heat. Add chicken and sear until well browned on both sides (appx 5 minutes per side).

In second skillet, heat one tablespoon oil olive, simmer tomatoes, garlic, parsley, basil, sugar, salt and pepper over low heat until sauce is cooked.

Toss cooked chicken into sauce; keep warm.

Cook linguini according to package directions.

Spoon sauce over hot linguini and sprinkle with cheese.

Peanut Butter Cup Cheesecake

Source: Kappa House		**Type:** Cakes
Origin:		**Category:** Dessert

Quantity	Measure	Item
3/4	Cup	**Graham Cracker Crumbs**
2	Tablespoon	**Sugar**
2	Tablespoon	**Melted Butter**
3/4	Cup	**Creamy Peanut Butter**
1	Cup	**Sour Cream**
3/4	Cup	**Sugar**
2		**Eggs - lightly beaten**
1 1/2	Teaspoon	**Vanilla**
3/4	Cup	**Hot Fudge Sauce**
6		**Peanut Butter Cups; cut into wedges**
3	8 ounce	**Cream cheese**

Instructions:

Combine cracker crumbs, butter and sugar; press onto the bottom of a 9" spring form pan coated with baking spray (or put in 9 x 13 dish. Bake for 10 minutes on 350. Cool.

Put peanut butter in microwave for 30 seconds or until softened. Spread over crust to 1" from edges.

In large bowl, beat cream cheese, sour cream and sugar until smooth. Add eggs, beat until well blended. Add vanilla. Save 1 cup of batter. Pour remaining over peanut butter layer.

In microwave heat 1/4 cup hot fudge topping on high for 30 seconds or until thin. Fold into reserved cream cheese mixture. Carefully pour over filling; cut thru with a knife to swirl.

Return to oven for 50-60 minutes or until center is almost set.

Cool for 1 hour or longer.

Microwave remaining fudge topping of high for 30 seconds or until warmed. Spread over cheesecake. Garnish with peanut butter cups.

Refrigerated overnight.

Peanut Butter Popcorn

Source: Pat		**Type:** Miscellaneous
Origin: US		**Category:** Snack

Quantity	Measure	Item
5	Cup	Popped Popcorn
1	Cup	Dry roasted peanut
1/2	Cup	Sugar
1/2	Cup	Light corn syrup
1/2	Cup	Peanut butter (smooth or chunky)
1/2	Teaspoon	Vanilla

Instructions:

Place popcorn and peanuts in a large bowl; set aside.

In a large saucepan over medium heat, bring sugar and corn syrup to a rolling boil, stirring occasionally.

Remove from heat; stir in peanut butter and vanilla.

Pour quickly over popcorn mixture and mix well.

Let stand at room temperature until firm.

Peanutty Squares

Source: Pat	**Type:** Cookies
Origin: US	**Category:** Dessert

Quantity	Measure	Item
1	Cup	Peanut Butter
2	Cup	Marshmallow Crème
1		Stick Butter
4	Cup	Cheerios
1	Cup	Brown Sugar
1	Cup	Peanuts

Instructions:

Melt over medium heat peanut butter, marshmallow crème, and butter.

Add Cheerios. Stir in one cup of brown sugar and peanuts.

Pat into buttered 9x13 pan.

Cool cut into squares.

Pecan Caramels

Source: Pat
Origin: US

Type: Candy
Category: Dessert

Quantity	Measure	Item
2	Teaspoon	Butter
1	Cup	Butter
1 1/4	Cups	Packed brown sugar
1 1/4	Cups	Sugar
2	Cups	Heavy Whipping Cream Divided
2	pounds	Chopped pecans
1	Teaspoon	Vanilla
1	Cup	Dark corn syrup

Instructions:

Line a 13 x 9 pan with foil: grease the foil with 2 tsp butter and set aside.

In a large heavy saucepan, combine the sugar, corn syrup, 1 cup cream and the 1 cup butter.

Cook and stir over medium heat until sugar is dissolved.

Bring to a boil.

Slowing stir in remaining cream.

Cook without stirring until a candy thermometer reads 245 (firm ball stage).

Remove from heat; stir in pecans and vanilla.

Pour into prepared pan.

Let stand until firm.

Using foil, lift candy out of pan.

Discard foil; cut into 1" squares

Pecan Crumble Sweet Potato Casserole

Source: BeckiDroege	**Type:** Vegetable
Origin:	**Category:** Side Dish

Quantity	Measure	Item
3	Large	Sweet potatoes
1/2	Cup	Butter (divided)
1	Cup	Crushed graham crackers
1/2	Cup	Packed brown sugar
1	Teaspoon	Ground cinnamon
1/2	Teaspoon	Salt
1/4	Teaspoon	Ground black pepper

Instructions:

Preheat oven 350

Prick sweet potatoes with fork

Microwave on high for 18-20 minutes

Melt 5 T butter

Combine melted butter, graham crackers, pecans, brown sugar & cinnamon

Peel sweet potatoes and mash in a large bowl with remaining butter, salt & pepper put in

8x8 and top with pecan mixture

Bake 20-25 minutes until golden brown

Peppermint Cookie Cups

Source: Becki		**Type:** Cookies
Origin: Unknown		**Category:** Dessert

Quantity	Measure	Item
		Chocolate chips, M & M's, or crushed peppermint candy
1	batch	Chocolate chip cookie dough (or refrigerated tube)
8	Ounce	Cream cheese
4	Tablespoon	Butter
1	Teaspoon	Peppermint extract
2 1/2	Cup	Powder sugar

Instructions:

Press cookie dough into the bottom and up the sides of an ungreased muffin pan.

Bake at 350 for 10 minutes or until lightly browned.

Using end of wooden spoon reshape the puffed cookie cups and cool for 5 minutes.

Remove to a wire rack to cool completely.

Beat the cream cheese, butter, peppermint extract until blended.

Gradually add sugar

Spoon into cookie cups

Add decorations of your choice to top

Store in refrigerator

Variations: Try sugar cookie dough with almond extract with a strawberry on top

Pepperoni Pizza

Source:	**Type:** Meat
Origin:	**Category:** Entree

Quantity	Measure	Item
2	Pound	Ground beef
1	Portion	Hot Italian Sausage
1	Large	Onion; sliced
1	Large	Green pepper; chopped
4	Clove	Garlic; minced
1	16 ounce	jar Salsa
1	16 ounce	can Hot chili beans; undrained
1	16 ounce	can Kidney beans; drained and rinsed
1	12 ounce	Pizza Sauce
1	8 ounce	Sliced pepperoni, halved
1	Cup	Water
1/2	Teaspoon	Salt
1/2	Teaspoon	Pepper
3	Cup	Mozzarella cheese; shredded

Instructions:

Cook beef, sausage, onion, pepper, and garlic until browned; drain

Stir in Salsa, beans, pizza sauce, pepperoni, water, chili powder, salt and pepper

Bring to a boil. Reduce heat; cover and simmer for 20 minutes

Sprinkle serving with cheese.

Pepperoni Pizzazz

Source: Becki Schilling Droege
Origin:

Type: Pasta
Category: Entree

Description: Can be made the night before and then baked for a quicker dinner or lunch.

Quantity	Measure	Item
8	Ounce	Rigatoni pasta; cooked
28	Ounce	Spaghetti sauce
4 1/2	Ounce	Sliced mushroom
8	Ounce	Pepperoni
1/2	Cup	Green pepper; chopped
1/2	Cup	Onion; Chopped
1/2	Cup	Parmesan cheese
1/2	Teaspoon	Garlic powder
1/2	Teaspoon	Salt
1/4	Teaspoon	Pepper
1/4	Teaspoon	Red pepper flakes
8	Ounce	Tomato sauce
8	Ounce	Mozzarella Cheese

Instructions:

Combine 2 1/3 cup spaghetti sauce, mushrooms, pepperoni, green pepper, onion, parm cheese and all spices.

Add pasta and mix well.

Put in greased 3 quart baking dish

Combine the tomato sauce and remaining spag sauce; pour over top.

Cover and bake at 350 for 40-45 minutes; until bubbly.

Sprinkle with cheese and bake uncovered additional 5-10 minutes until cheese is melted.

Let stand 5 minutes before serving.

Pie Crust

Source: Grandma Burger
Origin:

Type: Miscellaneous
Category: Dessert

Description: I know this recipe was in Volume 1, but as I was going thru my grandmother's recipes, I found an interesting card that I will share with you. The top of the recipe card simply said PASTRY. Pastry is a mixture of flour, shortening and liquid. When served it should be flaky, light and tender. The lightness depends upon the air enclosed in it. It's flakiness depends upon the amount of shortening and the method of mixing. There are three kinds of pastry. 1. Plain pastry in which the shortening is cut in or worked in with the tips of the fingers. 2. Puff pastry in which the chilled shortening is mixed by rolling and folding. 3. Flakey pastry in which the shortening is mixed in by using both the above methods.

Quantity	Measure	Item
2/3	Cup	Crisco
2	Cup	Flour
6	Tablespoon	Cold Water
1	Teaspoon	Salt

Instructions:

Put all these ingredients in a bowl and knead until mixed. (I use my hands).

Form into two equal balls.

Roll out using as much flour as you need so that it doesn't stick to the rolling pin or flat surface.

Fold in half and then slide into pie place.

Pizza Sandwich Loaf

Source: Kappa House
Origin: US

Type: Meat
Category: Sandwich

Quantity	Measure	Item
2	Loaves	Unsliced Italian bread (8 ounces each)
6	Tablespoon	Olive oil - divided
14.5	Ounce	Italian diced tomatoes - drained
6	Ounce	Tomato paste
6	Ounce	Canadian Bacon
3.5	Ounce	Pepperoni
1	Clove	Garlic
1/2	Teaspoon	Basil
1/2	Teaspoon	Oregano
1/8	Teaspoon	Pepper
1	Cup	Mozzarella Cheese
1/4	Cup	Parmesan Cheese

Instructions:

Cut bread length-wise and hollow out bottom portion.

Using 4 tablespoons of oil - brush the inside of the bread.

Bake at 350 for 5-10 minutes or until toasted.

In saucepan combine tomatoes, paste, meat, and spices.

Bring to a boil over medium heat.

Reduce heat and simmer for 10 minutes.

Stir in cheeses.

Spoon sauce into bread shells.

Replace top and brush with remaining oil.

Bake at 350 for 15 minutes or until heated thru.

Variations: Instead of meat, you can use spinach and mushrooms.

Popcorn Nut Crunch

Source: Pat	**Type:** Miscellaneous
Origin: US	**Category:** Snack

Description: Nuts need to be toasted before assembling with popcorn

Quantity	Measure	Item
2	Quarts	Popped popcorn
1	Cup	Blanched whole almonds, toasted
1	Cup	Each: pecan halves, cashews, Brazil nuts, and hazelnuts, toasted
1 1/2	Cup	Sugar
1	Cup	Dark corn syrup
1/2	Cup	Butter
1	Teaspoon	Vanilla
1/2	Teaspoon	Cinnamon

Instructions:

Place popcorn and nuts in a lightly greased 5 quart oven pan.

Bake at 250 for 20 minutes.

In medium saucepan combine: sugar, corn syrup and butter; bring to a boil over medium heat, stirring constantly.

Cook without stirring, until a candy thermometer reads 290 (soft crack stage).

Remove from heat; stir in vanilla and cinnamon.

Pour a small amount at a time over the popcorn mixture, stirring until the mixture is well coated.

Pork Chops and Rice

Source: Grandma Burger
Origin:

Type: Meat
Category: Entree

Description: Nuts A slow oven is 325. The best way to cook pork is low and slow. As for the fat - try your favorite oil. The raw rice is uncooked rice.

Quantity	Measure	Item
		Enough hot water to cover chops
6		Pork Chops
6	Tablespoon	Raw rice
3		Onion slices
6	Slices	Green pepper
2	Cup	Canned tomatoes

Instructions:

Wipe chops with a damp cloth to free of all splinters of bone

Season with salt and pepper and dredge lightly with flour.

Into a heavy skillet, heat 2 tablespoons of fat and brown chops lightly.

Then place meat in casserole with a slice of onion and pepper on each chop.

Add a tablespoon of rice to each chop, placing it in a mound on top.

Add canned or cooked tomatoes and hot water.

Cover closely and bake in a slow oven for at least 2 hours.

Lift chops fro dish to each plate

Pot Roast

Source: Kappa House
Origin: US

Type: Meat
Category: Entree

Description: You do not need a Dutch oven. You can make this stove top with any large pot. Actually a Dutch oven is just a cover pot. Years ago they were made out of cast iron.

Quantity	Measure	Item
3	Pound	Beef Sirloin Tip Roast
1	Tablespoon	Oil
1	14 1/2 ounce	Beef Broth
2	Tablespoon	Cider Vinegar
2	Clove	Garlic
1 /2	Teaspoon	Basil
1/4	Teaspoon	Thyme
1	Small	Cabbage; cut into chunks
3	Medium	Carrots; cut into chunks
4	Medium	Potatoes; cut into quarters
2	Medium	Onions; cut into chunks
1/2	Teaspoon	Salt
1/2	Teaspoon	Pepper
1/4	Cup	Flour
1/4	Cup	Cold water

Instructions:

In a Dutch oven, brown roast on all sides in oil over medium heat; drain.

Add broth. Pour vinegar over meat.

Sprinkle with garlic, basil and thyme.

Bring to a boil. Reduce heat; cover and simmer for 2 hours; turning roast occasionally.

Add water if needed. Add veggies to pan. Sprinkle with salt and pepper.

Cover and simmer for 35-45 minutes or until veggies and meat are tender.

For gravy: remove meat and veggies from pan.

Mix flour and cold water until smooth and gradually add to broth.

Bring to a boil and stir until thick.

Pulled Chicken Sandwiches

Source: Kappa House	**Type:** Poultry	
Origin: US	**Category:** Sandwich	

Quantity	Measure	Item
		Bread/bagette/or bun of choice
3	Pound	Boneless, skinless, chicken thighs
1		Onion
1/2	Cup	BBQ Sauce - your favorite kind
1/4	Cup	Water
1	Tablespoon	Brown sugar
4	Slices	American Cheese

Instructions:

Cook chicken and let cool and shred.

In skillet combine chicken, onion, BBQ sauce, water and brown sugar. Bring to a boil and simmer for about 10 minutes until sauce has thicken a little.

Serve with the bread of choice and cheese.

Pumpkin Butterscotch Cookies

Source: Katy Freeman	**Type:** Cookies	
Origin:	**Category:** Dessert	

Quantity	Measure	Item
2	Cup	Flour
1 1/2	Teaspoon	Baking powder
1	Teaspoon	Baking soda
1/2	Teaspoon	Salt
1	Teaspoon	Cinnamon
2		Eggs
1	Cup	Sugar
1/2	Cup	Vegetable oil
1	Cup	Pumpkin puree
1	Teaspoon	Vanilla
1	Cup	Butterscotch chips

Instructions:

Preheat oven to 325. Line two baking sheets with parchment paper.

In a small bowl combine flour, baking powder, baking soda, salt and cinnamon; whisk to blend.

Combine eggs and sugar and add to the flour mixture. Then beat on medium-high speed until smooth and light in color, about 1 minute.

Blend in the oil, pumpkin puree and vanilla extract until well combined.

With the mixer on low speed, mix in the dry ingredients until blended.

Gently fold in butterscotch chips.

Drop mounds of dough on the cookie sheets.

Bake about 14-16 minutes (rotating midway thru).

Toothpick will come out clean.

Allow to cool 5-10 minutes before transferring to wire rack to cool completely.

Pumpkin Cheesecake

Source: Kappa House	**Type:** Cakes	
Origin:	**Category:** Dessert	

Quantity	Measure	Item
		Crust
2	Cup	Crust cinnamon graham cracker (about 10 ounce box)
1/4	Cup	Butter
		Filling
4	8 ounce	Cream cheese; softened
1 1/2	Cup	Sugar
4		Egg
1	Can 14 1/2 oz	Canned pumpkin
2	Teaspoon	Pumpkin pie spice
		Spiced Caramel-Rum Sauce
1/3	Cup	Packed brown sugar
1/3	Cup	Dark Karo syrup
2	Tablespoon	Butter
1/3	Cup	Whipping cream
1/4	Teaspoon	Rum extract

Instructions:

Heat oven to 300. Spray 9" spring form pan with cooking spray.

Mix crust ingredients and press mixture into bottom and 1" up sides. Bake 8-10 minutes or until set. Cool 5 minutes. To minimize cracking, place a shallow pan half full of hot water onto lower rack.

In large bowl, beat cream cheese and granulated sugar with electric mixer until light and fluffy. Beat in eggs, one at a time just until blended. Spoon 3 cups of mixture onto crust; spread evenly. To remaining cream cheese mixture, add pumpkin and pumpkin pie spice. mix until smooth. Spoon over mixture in pan.

Bake 1 hour and 15 minutes or until edge of cheese cake is set at a least 2" from edge of pan and center of cheesecake still jiggles slightly.

Turn off oven and crack door. Let cheesecake remain in oven for 30 minutes. Then cool for 30 minutes.

Cover loosely; refrigerate at least 6 hours, but no longer than 24 hours.

In small saucepan heat brown sugar, corn syrup and 2 tablespoons butter to boiling over medium-high heat, stirring constantly. Boil 5 minutes. Stir in whipping cream; heat to boiling.

Remove from heat and stir in rum.

Just before serving run a small metal spatula around edge of pan; carefully remove sides of pan.

Top individual slices with warm sauce.

Cover and refrigerate any remaining cheesecake.

Pumpkin Cookies

Source: Kim Trejo	**Type:** Cookies
Origin:	**Category:** Dessert

Quantity	Measure	Item
		Sift together
2	Cup	Flour
1	Teaspoon	Baking powder
1	Teaspoon	Baking soda
1	Teaspoon	Cinnamon
1/2	Teaspoon	Salt
		Cream together
1	Cup	Butter
1	Cup	Sugar
1	Cup	Canned Pumpkin
1	Teaspoon	Vanilla
1		Egg
		Powder sugar to thicken
		Candy corn to decorate
		Frosting
1/2	Cup	Brown sugar
4	Tablespoon	Milk
3	Tablespoon	Butter
		Bring to a boil
1	Teaspoon	Vanilla

Instructions:

After mixing together the flour mixture and the creamed mixture;

Bake at 375 for 8 - 10 minutes.

Let cookies cool.

Frost cookie and add candy corn when cool.

Pumpkin Dessert

Source: Becki Droege

Origin:

Type: Cakes

Category: Dessert

Quantity	Measure	Item
		Pecans
1	Large	Can Pumpkin
3		Egg
3	Teaspoon	Cinnamon
1	Can	Sweetened condensed milk
1	Cup	Sugar
		Yellow cake mix
1	stick	Butter

Instructions:

Mix first six ingredients.

Pour into 9 x 13 pan.

Sprinkle cake mix on top.

Pour melted butter over cake mix.

Put pecans on top.

Bake at 350 for 1 hour.

Ranch Dressing

Source: Pat	**Type:** Dressing	
Origin: US	**Category:** Miscellaneous	

Quantity	Measure	Item
1	Cup	Mayo (Hellman's)
1	Cup	Buttermilk
1	Package	Ranch buttermilk

Instructions:

Mix ingredients and store in refrigerator.

Roasted Tomatoes

Source: Pat	**Type:** Vegetable	
Origin:	**Category:** Side Dish	

Quantity	Measure	Item
		Olive Oil
		Salt
		Pepper
		Oregano
		Garlic
20-25		**Tomatoes**

Instructions:

Cubes the tomatoes and let drain in a colander.

After draining put in bowl and add all the other ingredients.

Bake in oven at 200 for 8-10 hours.

Santa Fe Cheese Soup

Source: Pam Elliott	**Type:**	
Origin: US Southwest	**Category:** Soup	

Quantity	Measure	Item
1	Pound	Ground Beef (browned and drained)
1	Can	15 1/4 oz Whole Kernel Corn with liquid
1	Can 15 oz	Kidney Beans with liquid
1	Can 14 1/2 oz	Diced Fire Roasted Tomatoes with liquid
1	Can 14 1/2 oz	Mexican Style Stewed Tomatoes with liquid
1	envelope	Taco Seasoning Mix
1	Pound Velveeta Cheese,	Cubed

Instructions:

Combine all ingredients in 4 1/2 - 6 quart slow cooker.

Cover and cook on high for 3 hours or 4-5 hours on low.

Serve with corn chips

Variations:

If you don't like your soup as spicy, used regular diced and stewed tomatoes.

Saucy Pasta

Source:	Type: Pasta
Origin:	Category: Entree

Quantity	Measure	Item
1	Pound	Ground beef
1	Medium	Onion, chopped
3	Cup	Rotini pasta, uncooked
3 1/2	Cup	Water
1	26 ounce Jar	spaghetti sauce
1	Cup	Sliced mushrooms
1	Cup	Red peppers; chopped
1	Cup	Mozzarella cheese

Instructions:

Brown meat in large deep skillet, drain.

Add onions; cook until tender.

Add pasta, water and spaghetti sauce.

Bring to a boil, cover. Reduce heat to low, simmer for 15 minutes, stirring occasionally.

Add mushrooms and red peppers, cook 5 minutes.

Sprinkle with cheese.

Sausage Bread Pudding

Source: Becki Droege		**Type:** Meat
Origin:		**Category:** Entre

Description : This recipe was altered from a breakfast dish with ham. You can substitute the sausage for 8 ozs. of ham if you prefer.

Quantity	Measure	Item
8	ounces	French or Italian bread
3	Tablespoon	Butter
1	Pound	Sausage, browned
2	Cup	Sharp cheddar cheese
3		Eggs
2	cups	Milk
1	Teaspoon	Dry mustard
1/2	Teaspoon	Salt
1/2	Teaspoon	White pepper

Instructions:

Grease 11x7 dish

Spread 1 side of each bread slice with butter

Cut into cubes

Place in bottom of dish

Top with sausage

Sprinkle with cheese

Beat eggs and milk

Add mustard, salt and pepper

Pour over bread

Cover and refrigerate for 6 hours or overnight

Preheat oven to 350

Bake uncovered 45-50 minutes (until puffy and gold brown)

Serve immediately

Shrimp with Pesto and Spaghetti

Source: Kappa House	**Type:** Meat	
Origin:	**Category:** Entree	

Quantity	Measure	Item
8	Ounce	Uncooked Spaghetti
1	Cup	Basil Leaves
1/4	Cup	Lemon Juice
2	Clove	Garlic
3	Tablespoon	Olive Oil
1/2	Teaspoon	Salt
1	Pound	Asparagus, trimmed and cut into 2" pieces
3/4	Pound	Shrimp; peeled and deveined
1/5	Teaspoon	Crushed red pepper flakes

Instructions:

Cook Spaghetti according to package directions.

In blender or food processor, combine the basil, lemon juice, garlic, 1 tablespoon oil and salt; cover and process until smooth.

In a large skillet sauté asparagus in remaining oil until crisp tender.

Add the shrimp and pepper flakes.

Cook and stir until shrimp turns pink.

Place cooked spaghetti in large bowl.

Coat with basil mixture, add shrimp mixture; mix well.

Sloppy Joe

Source: Kappa House	**Type:** Meat	
Origin: US	**Category:** Sandwich	

Quantity	Measure	Item
		Buns
2	pounds	Ground Beef
1	Cup	Ketchup
1	Cup	KC Master BBQ Sauce
2	Tablespoon	Brown Sugar
2	Teaspoon	Worcestershire sauce
2	Teaspoon	Mustard
1/2	Teaspoon	Garlic Powder
1/2	Teaspoon	Onion Powder
1/2	Teaspoon	Salt

Instructions:

Brown ground beef; drain.

Stir in remaining ingredients.

Bring to a boil.

Reduce heat; cover and simmer for 30-40 minutes.

Serve on buns.

Snickers Salad

Source: Becki Droege		**Type:** Candy
Origin:		**Category:** Dessert

Description : Someone brought this Labor Day Saturday and it was gone so fast that I didn't even get to try it but I licked the sides and had to have the recipe. You can be made ahead; do everything but the apples. Chill over night. Cut and fold in apples when ready to serve.

Quantity	Measure	Item
1	8 ounce	Cream cheese softened
1	Cup	Powder sugar
1	12 ounce	Cool Whip
6	Snicker Bars;	chopped (freezing for 1/2 hour makes them easier to chop).
6		Tart Apples

Instructions:

Combine cream cheese with sugar until well blended.

Fold in cool whip.

Add chopped candy bars and apples.

Chill 1 hour before serving.

Southwest Frito Pie

Source:	**Type:** Meat	
Origin: US Southwest	**Category:** Entree	

Quantity	Measure	Item
		Sour cream and minced cilantro; optional
2	Pound	Ground Beef
3	Tablespoon	Chili powder
2	Tablespoon	Flour
1	Teaspoon	Salt
1	Teaspoon	Garlic powder
2	Cup	Water
1	15 ounce can	Pinto bean; rinsed and drained
4 1/2	Cup	Corn chips
2	Cup	Shredded lettuce
1 1/2	Cup	Cheddar cheese; shredded
1/4	Cup	Tomatoes; chopped
6	Tablespoon	Chopped onion

Instructions:

Cook beef until no longer pink; drain. Stir in chili powder, flour, salt, and garlic powder until blended; gradually stir in water.

Add beans. Bring to a boil. Reduce heat; simmer uncover 12-15 minutes or until thickened. Stirring occasionally.

Divide Chips among 6 serving bowls. Top with beef mixture, lettuce, cheese, tomatoes, and onion.

Garnish with sour cream and cilantro if desired.

Spiced Nuts

Source: Ellen Dodd		**Type:** Miscellaneous
Origin:		**Category:** Snack

Quantity	Measure	Item
3	Cup	Roasted pecans
1	Cup	Shelled pistachios
2	Cup	Almond
1/2	Teaspoon	Coriander
1/2	Teaspoon	Cumin
3	Tablespoon	Butter
2	Tablespoon	Brown sugar
1/2	Teaspoon	Cayenne pepper
1 1/2	Teaspoon	Salt
1/2	Teaspoon	Worcestershire sauce

Instructions:

Preheat oven to 325.

Place nuts on a rimmed baking sheet.

Place in oven, shaking the sheet several times during baking; about 10-15 minutes.

In a small skillet over low heat, add coriander, cumin, butter, brown sugar,

Worcestershire sauce, cayenne and salt.

Stir until the butter melts and sugar dissolved.

Place nuts in bowl, pour the warm spiced butter over the nuts; stir until well coated.

Let cool completely before serving.

Store in airtight container.

Spiced Pecans

Source: Ellen Dodd
Origin:

Type: Miscellaneous
Category: Snack

Quantity	Measure	Item
3	Cup	Pecan halves
2	Tablespoon	Butter, melted
1	Large	Egg White
2	Tablespoon	Sugar
1	Teaspoon	Cinnamon
1/4	Teaspoon	Cloves
1/4	Teaspoon	allspice
1 1/2	Teaspoon	Red hot pepper sauce

Instructions:

Heat oven to 350.

On large baking sheet, stir together pecans and butter.

Bake pecans 5 to 10 minutes or until lightly browned.

Cool for appx 10 minutes.

In small bowl, combine egg white, sugar, cinnamon, cloves, allspice and pepper sauce; stir into browned pecans.

Bake another 5 to 8 minutes longer, stirring occasionally, until mixture hardens.

Cool pecans to room temperature.

Stir to break up nuts.

Serve

Spicy Oyster Crackers

Source: Becki Schilling Droege
Origin:

Type: Miscellaneous
Category: Snack

Quantity	Measure	Item
14	Ounce	Oyster Crackers
1/2	Cup	Corn Oil
1/2	Teaspoon	Dill weed
1/2	Teaspoon	Parsley flakes
1/2	Teaspoon	Garlic powder
1	Package	Ranch dressing

Instructions:

Heat oil for about 30 seconds in microwave.

Add all spices, toss with crackers,

Layout to air dry.

Store in tight container.

Spicy Vanilla Pecans

Source: Elen Dodd		**Type:** Miscellaneous
Origin:		**Category:** Snack

Quantity	Measure	Item
1	Pound	Pecan Halves
6	Cup	Water
1/2	Cup	Sugar
3	Tablespoon	Butter; melted
1	Teaspoon	Corn syrup
1	Teaspoon	Vanilla
1/4	Teaspoon	Salt
1/4	Teaspoon	Cinnamon
1/4	Teaspoon	Nutmeg
1/4	Teaspoon	Allspice
1/8	Teaspoon	Pepper

Instructions:

Boil pecans in water for one minute; drain,

Immediately toss pecans in a large bowl with sugar, butter, corn syrup and vanilla.

Cover bowl and let sit for 12-24 hours.

Place pecans on an ungreased jelly-roll pan.

Bake at 325 for 30 minutes, stirring every 5 minutes.

While pecans are baking, combine remaining ingredients in a large bowl.

After baking pecans, immediately toss them with spices until well coated

Spread pecans on the jelly-roll pan in a single layer to allow to cool.

Sticky Toffee

Source: Princess Kate	**Type:** Cakes	
Origin: England	**Category:** Dessert	

Description: I fell in love with this dessert in 2005 when I spent several weeks in the UK. That winter Xmas was spent in the Grand Caymans, which is a British West Indies island. One of the waiters got his grandmother's recipe and made it for us. It is still on the dessert menu at The Marriot Beach Resort on Seven Mile Beach. While this is not the same recipe, I copied this out of People Magazine. Very Yummy. Also, I have been know to buy caramel sauce or toffee sauce instead of making it.

Quantity	Measure	Item
8	Ounce	Pitted dates, chopped
1 1/4	Cup	Boiling water
1/3	Cup	Butter; softened
		(3.5 tbsp for batter, rest to butter the pan)
1	Cup	Dark brown sugar
2		Egg
2	Tablespoon	Black Treacle or dark molasses
1	Tablespoon	Lyle's Golden Syrup
1	Teaspoon	Vanilla
2	Cup	Self rising cake flour
1	Tablespoon	Baking soda.
		Toffee Sauce
1/2	Cup	Sugar
7	Tablespoon	Butter
6	Ounce	English cream

Instructions:

In a bowl, cover dates with boiling water. Set aside.

Preheat oven to 375. Place a roasting pan with water in the oven.

Butter a 9x9 pan.

Dust with flour.

Mix 3.5 tablespoons butter with sugar until combined (I use electric mixer). Beat in eggs, one at a time, then add treacle, Golden Syrup and vanilla. Mix until just combined. On low speed add flour.

In food processor; puree dates. Stir in baking soda and mix into batter.

Pour into prepared pan. Place in roasting pan and bake for 35 minutes until just firm on top.

In a sauce pan over medium heat, melt sugar and butter until mixture turns a deep amber color.

Watch closely so it doesn't burn. Slowly mix in double cream. Once all the cream is added cook mixture until thick.

Cut cake into squares and serve with toffee sauce and ice cream.

Strawberry Bread

Source:	**Type:** Fruit	
Origin:	**Category:** Breads	

Quantity	Measure	Item
2		Eggs
1/2	Cup	Vegetable oil
1	Cup	Sugar
1/2	Teaspoon	Vanilla
1/2	Teaspoon	Almond extract
1 2/3	Cup	Flour
1/2	Teaspoon	Baking soda
1/2	Teaspoon	Baking powder
1/2	Teaspoon	Salt
1 1/2	Cup	Chopped strawberries – fresh or frozen and lightly drained
1/2	Cup	Nuts- your choice

Instructions:

Heat oven to 350 degrees.

Beat eggs until foamy.

Add oil, sugar, vanilla, almond and mix well.

Stir well or sift together flour, baking soda, powder, and salt.

Add to liquid mixture and stir until moistened.

Add strawberries and nuts and mix lightly

Don't over mix.

Pour into greased 9 x 5 loaf pan and bake 50-60 minutes until nicely browned.

Strawberry Lemon Ade

Source: Pat	**Type:** Fruit	
Origin: US	**Category:** Beverage	

Quantity	Measure	Item
1	Can	Frozen Lemonade
1	Pint	Fresh or frozen Strawberries (blended)
1	8 ounce	Club Soda or Sierra Mist
3	Can	Water - from frozen lemonade can
1	Cup	Sugar

Instructions:

Blend lemonade and strawberries.

Add water, soda, sugar.

Serve over ice.

String Cheese Manicotti

Source: Becki	**Type:** Pasta	
Origin: Italy	**Category:** Entree	

Quantity	Measure	Item
1	8 oz. pkg	Manicotti shells
1	Pound	Ground beef, chicken, Italian sausage or veggies for meatless
1/2	Cup	Chopped onion
1	26 ounce	Spaghetti sauce
14	1ounce	Pieces string cheese
1 1/2	Cup	Shredded mozzarella cheese

Instructions:

Cook manicotti according to package directions.

In a large skillet cook meat and onions over medium heat until meat is done.

Drain, stir in spaghetti sauce.

Spread half the meat sauce onto a greased 9 x 13.

Stuff each shell with a piece of string cheese and place over meat.

Top the manicotti mixture with remaining sauce.

Cover and bake at 350 for 24-30 minutes or until heated through.

Sprinkle with mozzarella cheese and return to oven uncovered until cheese melts (5-10 minutes).

Sun-Dried Tomato and Olive Pesto

Source: Kappa House	**Type:** Pasta
Origin:	**Category:** Entree

Description: Since there is an abundance of tomatoes in the summer, I have been roasting them myself and then making the pesto. Look for roasted tomatoes recipe.

Quantity	Measure	Item
2/3	Cup	Oil packed Sun Dried Tomato
3/4	Cup	Basil
2/3	Cup	Black Olives
1/2	Cup	Pine nuts or Walnuts
2	Clove	Garlic
1/2	Cup	Parmesan
12	Ounce	Penne Pasta

Instructions:

Cook pasta according to package directions.

Meanwhile, blend the tomatoes, garlic, basil, olives, nuts and parmesan in food processor.

If needed add a little more olive oil.

Toss the pasta and pesto together and season with salt and pepper.

Sun-Dried Tomato Hummus

Source: Kappa House	**Type:** Vegetable	
Origin:	**Category:** Miscellaneous	

Quantity	Measure	Item
		Chopped fresh basil
		Chips or veggies.
2	15 ounce	can Garbanzo or chickpeas, rinsed and drained
1	7 ounce jar	Oil packed Sun-dried tomatoes; undrained
2/3	Cup	Water
3	Tablespoon	Olive oil
2	Clove	Garlic
1	Teaspoon	Crushed red pepper flakes
1/2	Teaspoon	Salt
1/4	Teaspoon	Pepper

Instructions:

In food processor, combine the beans, tomatoes, water, oil, garlic, pepper flakes, salt and pepper.

Process until well blended.

Place in bowl and sprinkle with basil.

Serves with chips or veggies.

Sweet Potato and Black Bean Chili

Source: Kappa House	**Type:** Vegetable
Origin:	**Category:** Soup

Quantity	Measure	Item
3	Large	Sweet potatoes, peeled and cut into 1/2" cubes
1	Large	Onion
1	Tablespoon	Olive oil
2	Tablespoon	Chili powder
3	Clove	Garlic, minced
1	Teaspoon	Cumin
1/4	Teaspoon	Cayenne pepper
2	15 ounce can	Black beans, rinsed and drained
1	28 ounce can	Dice tomatoes, undrained
1/4	Cup	Brewed coffee
2	Tablespoon	Honey
1/2	Teaspoon	Salt
1/4	Teaspoon	Pepper
1/2	Cup	Shredded Monterey Jack cheese

Instructions:

Sauté sweet potatoes and onion in large pot in oil until crisp-tender.

Add chili powder, garlic cumin, and cayenne; cook 1 minute longer.

Stir in beans, tomatoes, coffee, honey, salt and pepper.

Bring to a boil.

Reduce heat and simmer for 30-35 minutes or until sweet potatoes are tender.

Sprinkle with cheese.

Sweet Potato Soup

Source:	**Type:** Vegetable
Origin:	**Category:** Soup

Description: Perfect with a salad and yummy bread.

Quantity	Measure	Item
1		Leek, halved, rinsed and thinly sliced
2	stalks	Celery
1	Tablespoon	Butter
2	Large Sweet potatoes,	peeled and cut into 2" pieces
4	Cup	Chicken or vegetable broth
		Salt and pepper to taste
1/2	Cup	Toasted and chopped pecans; optional

Instructions:

Sauté leek and celery in a large saucepan over medium heat in the butter for appx 3 minutes

Add sweet potatoes and broth.

Bring to a boil.

Reduce heat, cover and simmer about 30 minutes.

Puree the soup in a food processor.

Return to pan and season with salt and pepper.

Garnish with pecans.

Taco Cornbread Pizza

Source: Becki Schilling Droege
Origin:

Type: Meat
Category: Entree

Description: Use any taco topping that you like.

Quantity	Measure	Item
		Taco Toppings
8.5	Ounce	Jiffy corn bread mix
		Buttermilk
1	Pound	Ground beef
1	Package	Taco seasoning
2	Cup	Shredded Cheese

Instructions:

Prepare corn meal using buttermilk in place of regular milk as directed on package

Spread into 12 pizza pan.

Bake at 400 for 8-10 minutes - lightly browned.

Brown ground beef and drain, add taco seasoning as directed on package.

Sprinkle with cheese and bake for 4-5 minutes until cheese melts.

Taco Dip

Source: Becki Schilling Droege
Origin:

Type: Meatless
Category: Appetizer

Description :simple and easy appetizer :)

Quantity	Measure	Item
		Lettuce
		Diced tomatoes
		Nachos
8 oz.		**Cream cheese**
1	**Cup**	**Sour cream**
1	**pkg**	**Taco seasoning**
1	**Jar**	**Taco sauce**
2	**Cup**	**Cheddar cheese**

Instructions:

Mix 1st three ingredients together until smooth

Spread in a dish

Top with taco sauce, lettuce, tomatoes and cheese

Serve with nachos

Taco Mac

Source: Becki Droege
Origin:

Type: Meat
Category: Entree

Description: I always double this recipe to feed my family and it totally kid friendly

Quantity	Measure	Item
1	Package	Shells and Cheese
1	Pound	Ground beef
1	Package	Taco seasoning
3/4	Cup	Sour cream
2	Cup	Cheddar cheese
1	Cup	Salsa

Instructions:

Make shells and cheese according to directions

Mix sour cream with it

Brown ground beef

Add taco seasoning according to directions

Place 1/2 of shells and cheese in 8x8

Put all of taco meat in

Top with 1/2 of cheese

Add the rest of the shells and cheese

Bake at 350 for 20 minutes

Top with the rest of cheese and bake until melted

Top with salsa and serve

Taco Salad

Source: Pat	**Type:** Salad	
Origin: US Southwest	**Category:** Entree	

Quantity	Measure	Item
1	Pound	Ground beef or chicken
1 1/2	Teaspoon	Chili Powder
1/2	Cup	Salsa
1/4	Cup	Salsa
1	10 oz Bag	Romaine Lettuce
2	Cup	Baked Tortilla Chips
1/3	Cup	Mexican Cheese
1	Medium	Ripe Avocado, pitted and cut into 1/2 in chunks
1/ 4	Cup	Sour Cream

Instructions:

Brown meat; stir in chili powder and cook 1 minute longer.

Add 1/2 cup salsa and cook 3-4 minutes.

Meanwhile divide lettuce among 4 plates.

Top each with meat mixture, tortilla chips, cheese, avocado, sour cream and remaining salsa.

Tilapia with Pesto

Source: Pat	**Type:** Meat
Origin:	**Category:** Entree

Description: You can also add a slice of tomato on top of the pesto is desired.

Quantity	Measure	Item
2	Bunches	Basil
1/2	Cup	Olive Oil
1	Clove	Garlic
1	Cup	Ricotta/Parmesan/Asaigo Chesse
1/2	Cup	Walnuts
4-6	Pieces	Tilapia

Instructions:

In food processor combine all ingredients except Tilapia. Add more Olive Oil if too thick, but you do want the pesto on the thicker side.

Arrange fish in baking dish

Spoon pesto sauce over each fillet of fish.

Bake at 350 for 20-30 minutes or until fish is cooked through.

You can add a little Mozzarella Cheese if desired.

Three Bean Salad

Source: Dorothy Tucker		**Type:** Vegetable
Origin: US		**Category:** Salad

Quantity	Measure	Item
1	Can	Green Beans
1	Can	Wax Beans
1	Can	Kidney Beans
1/2	Cup	Onion - chopped
1/2	Cup	Green pepper
1/2	Cup	Celery - chopped
2	Cup	Olive Oil
1/2	Cup	White Vinegar
3/4	Cup	Sugar

Instructions:

Drain beans and add onion, celery, and pepper.

Combine ingredients for dressing (oil, vinegar, and sugar) and pour over beans.

Mix well.

This is better prepared one day ahead.

Tomato Brushetta

Source:	**Type:** Miscellaneous	
Origin:	**Category:** Appetizer	

Description: This can be put together ahead of time and refrigerated.

Quantity	Measure	Item
4	Plum	tomatoes, seeded and chopped
1/2	Cup	Parmesan cheese; shredded
1/4	Cup	Basil; fresh and minced
3	Tablespoon	Olive oil
2	Tablespoon	Parsley; fresh and minced
3	Clove	Garlic; minced
2	Tablespoon	Balsamic vinegar
1/8	Teaspoon each	Pepper, salt and red pepper flakes
1	French baguette	cut into 1/2 inch slices
1/4	Cup	Butter softened
8	Ounce	Mozzarella cheese; sliced

Instructions:

Combine first 10 ingredients in a bowl.

Spread baguette slices with butter; top with a cheese slice. Place on ungreased baking sheet and broil for 3-4 minutes or until cheese is melted.

With slotted spoon, top each slice with about 1 tablespoon tomato mixture

Tomato Cobbler

Source: Kappa House   **Type:** Vegetable
Origin: **Category:** Entree

Quantity	Measure	Item
		Butter for baking dish
3	Pound	Tomatoes; cored and cut into wedges
1	Tablespoon	Corn Starch
		Coarse Salt and ground black pepper
1	Cup	Flour
1	Cup	Cornmeal
1 1/2	Teaspoon	Baking powder
1/4	Teaspoon	Baking Soda
4	Tablespoon	butter; cut into large pieces
1		Large Egg
3/4	Cup	Buttermilk

Instructions:

Preheat oven to 350. Butter a 2 quart baking dish; set aside

Place tomato wedges in a large bowl; sprinkle with cornstarch and season with salt and pepper.

Toss gently.

Place flour, cornmeal, baking powder, baking soda, and 1 teaspoon salt in food processor; pulse to combine. Add butter and pulse until mixture looks like coarse breadcrumbs. Add egg and buttermilk, pulse a few times until mixture comes together.

Gently toss tomato mixture again and spread over bottom of baking dish. Drop spoonfuls of the flour mixture on top' spreading evenly.

Bake 45-60 minutes or until golden brown.

Tomato Cream Soup

Source: Kappa House
Origin: US
Type: First Course
Category: Soup

Quantity	Measure	Item
2	Cup	Milk
1	14 1/2 ounce	Diced tomatoes undrained
1	8 oz. pkg	Cream cheese
1/4	Cup	Basil
1/2	Teaspoon	Salt
1/8	Teaspoon	Pepper

Instructions:

Place all ingredients in blender and process until smooth.

Transfer to large saucepan and heat through.

Tomato Mozzarella Salad

Source: Kappa House
Origin: US

Type: Salad
Category: Salad

Quantity	Measure	Item
1/4	Cup	Red wine vinegar
1	Clove	Garlic
1/2	Teaspoon	Salt
		Pepper to taste
2/3	Cup	Olive oil
1	Pint	Cherry tomatoes, halved
1 1/2	Cup	Cube mozzarella
1/4	Cup	Red onion
3	Tablespoon	Basil

Instructions:

Combine vinegar, garlic, salt, and pepper.

Whisk in oil until well blended.

Add remaining ingredients; toss to coat.

Cover and refrigerate for a least 1 hour, stirring occasionally.

Tropical Salad

Source: Kappa House
Origin:

Type: First Course
Category: Salad

Quantity	Measure	Item
1/2	Cup	Strawberry Yogurt
2	Tablespoon	Olive Oil
1 1/2	Teaspoon	White Balsamic Vinegar
5	Cup	Fresh Spring Mix Salad
1/2	Cup	Shredded Coconut
1/2	Cup	Strawberries; thinly sliced
1/2	Cup	Mandarin orange slices

Instructions:

Whisk yogurt, oil, and vinegar in a bowl until blended.

Toss the salad greens, coconut, strawberries and mandarin oranges in a bowl.

Add yogurt dressing and mix to coat.

Serve immediately.

Turtle Bars

Source: Becki Schilling Droege		**Type:** Candy
Origin:		**Category:** Dessert

Quantity	Measure	Item
		Chocolate frosting
		Box Graham crackers
1	Cup	Butter
1	Cup	Brown sugar
3/4	Cup	Chopped walnuts

Instructions:

Melt butter in pan and add sugar and nuts, bring to a boil, stirring constantly for 3 minutes

Line Crackers in a 9-x13 pan, pour butter mixture over it cracker.

Refrigerate until firm;

Frost

Back to fridge until ready to serve.

Vegetable Casserole

Source: Grandma Burger	**Type:** Vegetable	
Origin:	**Category:** Side Dish	

Quantity	Measure	Item
1 1/2	Cup	Carrots
1 10	ounce	Frozen Spinach
3	Tablespoon	Butter
3	Tablespoon	Flour
1 1/2	Cup	Milk
1	Cup	Shredded Sharp American Cheese
1/4	Teaspoon	Salt
		Pepper
1/2	Cup	Soft buttered bread crumbs

Instructions:

Preheat oven to 350.

Cook carrots and sliced onion in boiling salt water, until fork tender.

Cook spinach per package directions.

Drain veggies

Make Sauce:

Melt butter in saucepan, stirring in flour to make a smooth paste and then gradually adding milk, stirring until thick.

Remove from heat and add cheese, salt and pepper.

Stir until cheese melts.

Place 1/2 of spinach in ungreased casserole.

Cover with half the carrots and onions.

Top with half the cheese sauce.

Repeat layers.

Top with bread crumbs

Bake 15-20 minutes or until golden brown.

Vegetable Soup

Source: Nancy Mom Ziegler
Origin:

Type: Vegetable
Category: Soup

Quantity	Measure	Item
2	Pound	Beef shank or stewing beef
3	Tablespoon	Salt
4	Quart	Water
1	Teaspoon	Pepper
1/4	Cup	Sugar
3	Bay	Leaves
6	Medium	Red potatoes; cubed
1		Green pepper
2	Medium	Onions
5		Celery stalks
3	Large	Carrots or 12+ baby carrots; cup up
1	Cup	Grated cabbage
1	28 ounce can	Diced tomatoes
1	12 ounce bag	Green Beans;
1	12 ounce bag	Corn
1	12 ounce bag	Peas
1	12 ounce bag	Lima Beans

Instructions:

Put first six ingredients in large pot and bring to steam.

Simmer for 30 minutes at that temp.

Then turn on low for 2 hours or longer.

Add the next seven fresh ingredients.

Bring back to a high simmer for 15 minutes and then cook on low another 2+ hours.

Then add frozen vegetable and simmer for 30 minutes or longer.

Veggie Dip

Source: Pat		**Type:** Dips & Salsas
Origin:		**Category:** Miscellaneous

Quantity	Measure	Item
1	Cup	Hellman's Mayo
1	Cup	Cottage Cheese
1	Package	Hidden Valley Ranch Dressing

Instructions:

Mix all together and serve with veggie tray.

Vinaigrette Dressing

Source: Kappa House
Origin:

Type: Dressing
Category: Miscellaneous

Quantity	Measure	Item
6	Tablespoon	Olive Oil
1	Teaspoon	Garlic Powder
1	Teaspoon	Dried Oregano
1	Teaspoon	Dried Basil
1	Teaspoon	Dijon Mustard
1	Teaspoon	Lemon Juice
1 1/2	Cup	Red Wine Vinegar

Instructions:

Put all ingredients in a small bowl and whisk.